BUILDING WEBSITE WITH

JOOMLA! 1.5
IN 60 MINUTES

"You do not need to be a programmer; All you need is basic computer and internet knowledge to develop an impressive and high quality website in record time."

AK SHEHU

Copyright © 2014 by Ak Shehu.

ISBN: Hardcover   978-1-4828-9157-7
        Softcover   978-1-4828-9156-0
        Ebook   978-1-4828-9171-3

All rights reserved. No part of this book may be used or reproduced by any means, graphic, electronic, or mechanical, including photocopying, recording, taping or by any information storage retrieval system without the written permission of the publisher except in the case of brief quotations embodied in critical articles and reviews.

Because of the dynamic nature of the Internet, any web addresses or links contained in this book may have changed since publication and may no longer be valid. The views expressed in this work are solely those of the author and do not necessarily reflect the views of the publisher, and the publisher hereby disclaims any responsibility for them.

Limited Liability/Disclaimer of Warranty. Caveat emptor. No guarantees or claims of fitness with respect to accuracy and completeness are made by the author, the publisher, or other contributors. No warranty may be extended by salesperson or written sales materials. The strategies and advice contained herein may not be suitable for your situation. you should consult with a professional where appropriate. Neither the author nor publisher shall be liable for any loss of profit or other commercial damages, including but not limited to special, incidental, consequential, or other damages.

Dr. Ali Salman—Editor
Melanie Lee—Publishing Consultant

Emmanuel M. Espiritu II—Book Interior Designer
Shelly Edmunds—Publishing Service Associate
Charles Lee—Cover Designer 1
Cyril Villarante—Cover Designer 2

To order additional copies of this book, contact
Toll Free 800 101 2657 (Singapore)
Toll Free 1 800 81 7340 (Malaysia)
orders.singapore@partridgepublishing.com

www.partridgepublishing.com/singapore

Tip & Note: tells that further explanation and information is provided

Contents

Dedication v
Acknowledgement vi
Preface vii
Introduction viii

Chapter One 1
    Obtaining and Installing Joomla! 1
Chapter Two 23
    Creating Contents and Menus 23
Chapter Three 49
    Understanding Sections and Categories 49
Chapter Four 61
    Making your site Dynamic with Component,
    Modules & Plugins 61
Chapter Five 91
    Managing Front-end & Back-end Users 91
Chapter Six 107
    Working with the Media Manager 107
Chapter Seven 115
    Usability, Accessibility and Web Standards 115
Chapter Eight 127
    Using Templates and Extensions in Joomla! 127

Appendix 135
Appendix A: Exporting & Importing Joomla!
    Database from your computer 136
Appendix B: Key Resources 140
Appendix C: Look who's using Joomla! 142
About The Author 143

*I would like to dedicate this book to Noor A'an.
Without her love, support and patience, none of this would be possible.*

Acknowledgement

All praise is due to God, the creator of all that exists. Thanks to Him for the ability he gave me in writing this book.

When I first plan to write this book, I knew it would be a challenge to cover all important aspect of it and yet keep it from becoming too technical. It however took many people to get this book into your hands and I would like to extend my thanks to all.

I want to thank Dr. Ali Salman for his valuable input to this new book and to Ahmad Shehu for helping me to better explain the more obscure concepts. A special thanks to Abdul-Aziz Tanko, Riyaz Ahamed and Noor Farhan Najah Bt. Ramlee for their motivation and continued support while I crank out this Book.

I would like to extend a very special thank you to my Friend Muhammed Irfan Ishak for introducing me into Joomla!

I would like to also pay tribute to the Developers for their continued efforts in putting together the remarkable Content Management System that is Joomla! 1.5.

And finally to all my family and friends who always believed I could do it.

Preface

This book provides a broad and thorough introduction to Web design using Joomla! 1.5. It is intended primarily for any person with basic knowledge of computer and internet who wishes to develop a personal website or other kinds of websites. It presents a systematic account of the World Wide Web, which will serve as a foundation for anyone setting out on a career as a professional Web Designer.

I have written this book for you to learn Joomla! 1.5 as fast as possible, and thank you for deciding to read this book.

It is significant that this book is read cover-to-cover, and all you have to do is simply read a page, do what it says and go ahead. You will be a fluent Joomla! user after completing all the tasks in this book.

When I first came across Joomla! I found it difficult to install and difficult to learn how it works generally. It was even trickier to learn how to customize the site as per my requirement. In that period, there were many tutorials which explained different tasks, but not a single one explained how to install, administer or even modify Joomla! website to my needs. Thenceforth, I learned Joomla! in a more complex way by trying out different tutorials, trying different buttons in the administration, and seeing what happens. I gradually became facile in making and administrating Joomla! websites. It took me months going through all these processes.

I have now written this book in such a way that you will learn all that within minutes. If you have read this book three times cover-to-cover, you will be able to make any type of Joomla! website in Just 60 Minutes or less.

Introduction

In recent years, the internet has become one of the most booming industries and everyone wants to get in on it. Many companies have set up websites for people to visit and browse through their services or products. They have also posted the history of their company and their accomplishments so that people can be aware of them. However, if you were to venture into the internet market, would it not take a lot of time to get everything organized and at the same time, build the website? Relax, *Joomla!* is here to make it simple and easy in no time to develop and design your own website. In this case, you don't have to pay to get it done by a web design company.

However, as you might have already known, *Joomla!* is one of the Content Management Systems (CMS) and there are other CMS like Drupal, Wordpress, etc., but you may not be sure on which one to use. You don't have to worry; *Joomla!* makes life easy for you. This chapter will guide you through some easy key points to start building your Joomla! website. We shall be looking at the following things:

- Why do you need a website?

- Joomla! seems the right solution for me. How do I get started?

- What do you know about Joomla!?

- What is Content Management System (CMS)

- The Power of Joomla!

- Who Uses Joomla!?

- How do I install Joomla!?

- How should I set up my site?

- Picking a Template

- Organizing Content

- Creating Navigation

Why do you need a website?

You definitely should ask yourself, do I need a website? Yes, you might think! But why? If you don't have a clear goal for having or developing a website, your website will not be organized and will have no value. You must identify your goals or else you will be building site with no bearing; but what shall I use exactly for my website?

- Joomla!
- Wordpress
- Frog CMS
- Drupal
- Jumbo

To tell you the truth, Joomla! is an excellent solution for your website development and design. It has thousands of free extensions that will suit your needs in the development and design of your website. I strongly recommend you to go for it.

Joomla! seems the right solution for me. How do I get started?

Joomla! is free and anyone can use, share, and support it. To download the 1.5 version go to http://www.joomla.org/announcements/release-news/5393-joomla-1525-released.html for download. However, I will advice that you download the full package.

What do you know about Joomla!?

Joomla! is an award-winning content management system (CMS), which enables you to build websites and powerful online applications. Many aspects, including its ease-of-use and extensibility, have made Joomla! the most popular Website software available. Best of all, Joomla! is an open source solution that is freely available to everyone.

Joomla! is an "open source" Content Management System. An open Source means that anyone can contribute to the code, improve it, or distribute it. This means the platform is a living project being created and improved by a community of developers all over the world. However, a content management system uses a database to place content into designated places on the web page. It's dynamic and in real time. Joomla! is easy but powerful, cheap but not free.

The software itself is absolutely free, but there are some extensions that you might need to buy to really meet your website requirements. However, many extensions are free.

What is Content Management System (CMS)?

A content management system is software that keeps track of every piece of content on your website; much like your local public library keeps track of books and stores them. Content can be simple text, photos, music, video, documents, or just about anything you can think of. A major advantage of using a CMS is that it requires almost no technical skill or knowledge to manage.

The Power of Joomla!

Joomla! is used all over the world to power websites of all shapes and sizes. Joomla! can do the following:

- E-commerce and online reservations
- Government applications
- Small Business Web sites
- Non-profit and organizational Web sites
- Non-profit and organizational Web sites
- Community-based portals
- School and church Web sites
- Corporate Web sites or portals
- Online magazines, newspapers, and publications, and many more.

Who Uses Joomla!?

The following are just a few of the millions of organizations that use Joomla!:

- MTV Networks Quizilla (Social networking)— http://www.quizilla.com
- IHOP (Restaurant chain)— http://www.ihop.com
- Harvard University (Educational)— http://gsas.harvard.edu

- Outdoor Photographer (Magazine)-http://www.outdoorphotographer.com

- PlayShakespeare.com (Cultural)— http://www.playshakespeare.com

- And many more organizations using Joomla! to develop their website.

Joomla! is designed to be an easy-to-install software and you can set it up even if you're not an advanced user. Many Web hosting services offer a real time, single-click installation, getting your new site up and running in just a few minutes. Live!

Since Joomla! is so easy to use as a web designer or developer, you can quickly build sites for your clients. Then, with a minimal amount of instruction, you can empower your clients to easily manage their own sites themselves.

After mastering Joomla! you might want to develop website for some clients. However, your clients might need specialized functionalities and Joomla! is highly extensible, and thousands of extensions (most for free under the GPL license) are available in the Joomla! Extensions Directory. To see more on this, go to www.joomla.org

How do I set up My Joomla! Website?

Most people find it difficult to set up their site because it is one of the hardest parts of Joomla!. There are many options and can be overwhelming. Joomla! has three important elements which are:

1. **Template**-This gives the site a great look and with all the designs that are visible to visitors.

2. **Content**-This is the main area where information is displayed.

3. **Modules**-These contain the menus and can be set to any position within the template.

The picture shows what the three elements represent in Joomla!:

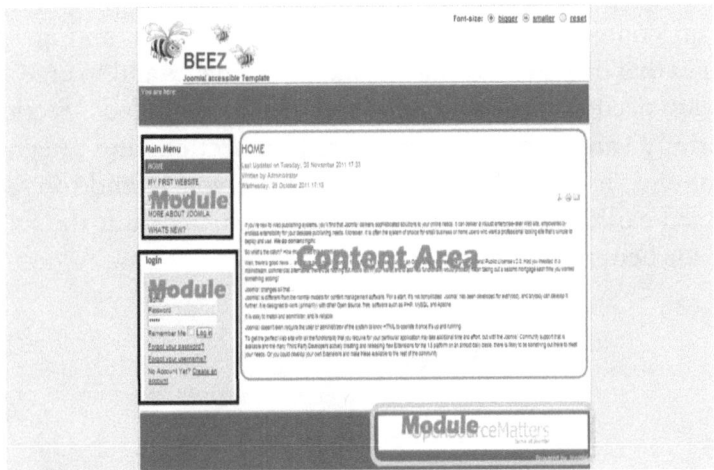

How do I pick a template in Joomla!?

To pick a template for your Joomla! Site, you will have to choose from any one of the following:

- Beez

- JA_Purity

- rhuk_milkway

Joomla! 1.5 always comes with three free templates. To get started, just use one of these, then you can graduate to a third-party template of which there are thousands available. You may choose to buy professional ones or use the free ones.

There are good free Joomla! templates on the internet; I would advise you to go through the free ones before considering buying a

xiii

commercial template. Always check the version of the template before using it (the focus of this book is Joomla! 1.5 version).

The Content

The main content of the site is made up of articles, and articles are WebPages that display information like text, images and so on. Content or articles need some containers and these are called "Section and Categories". Though not all websites require sections and categories for their content, it depends on the kind of site you intend to create. As mentioned earlier, you have to set your goal. Check out the following picture for better understanding:

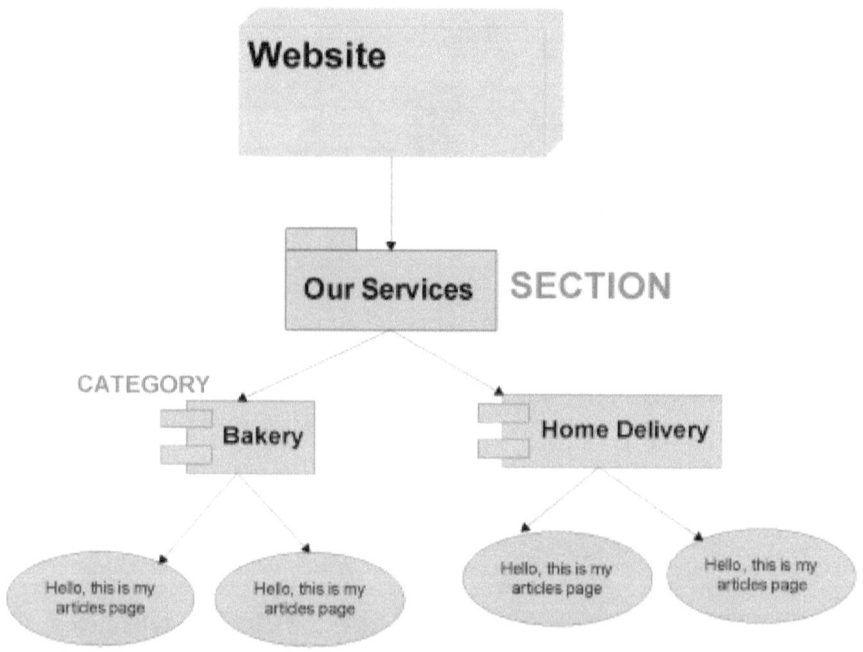

The picture signifies that the website contains sections, and sections contain categories. However, these categories can have many articles.

➤ You can have as many sections and categories you want on your website.

Creating Navigation

You will not be making any sense if your site doesn't have navigation. Visitors who will visit your site need to click through links, so it is indispensible to have links on your site. These can be the menu links; otherwise, nothing will be seen in your site. However, Joomla! has thousands of third-party extensions, ranging from online reservation, e-commerce, forums and many more. Some are free and some are commercial.

This section only highlights some of the key points that you need to know in order to master Joomla!. Read this book further to get more insight about developing websites with Joomla! 1.5 in minutes.

Chapter One

Obtaining and Installing Joomla!

Joomla! is a web application that was written using PHP (PHP is a programming language used for web application, it is an open source), and hence it needs a "web server" to run. To make a Joomla! website available on the World Wide Web, you need to host it on a web host. However, because you want to learn Joomla!, you can convert your own computer into a web server, and install Joomla on it. Hence, installing Joomla! on your computer requires you to do one basic thing. You will be shown how to do this.

Installing a Web Server—WAMP

WAMP means (Windows Apache MySQL PHP), it is a platform of Web development under Windows. Initially, installing a web server used to be a problem, especially because you had to manually configure it to run PHP. Not anymore, much thanks to WAMPthis is FREE software that installs an Apache Web Server, PHP and MySQL on your computer and configures these three to work together. All you have to do is download it and install!

There are different versions available for different operating system. However, you can download a copy of WAMP from this link (http://en.kioskea.net/download/download-1318-wamp-server).

Chapter One - Obtaining and Installing Joomla!

You are expected to run and install the web server as it is very simple to install, just follow the instructions. Most of the process is just to click Next until Finish. For more info on how to install the WAMP, please visit the following link (http://en.kioskea.net/download/download-1318-wamp-server).

Caution:

1. You must have a web server before you can install Joomla!

2. Make sure the WAMP server icon turns to white; it appears in the taskbar. If it's not turned on, you will not have access to your local site.

To start your server on your local PC, you have to double-click on the server application either on your desktop or at any location where you have saved it. It is advisable to have a shortcut icon on your desktop for easy access. Visit this link (http://en.kioskea.net/download/download-1318-wamp-server) to read more about WAMP Server.

Installing Joomla!

We have successfully installed WAMP server and now it's ready to use. You can download the 1.5 full packages from www.joomla.org. After doing so, unzip the folder and rename the unzipped folder to your website name (example: learnjoomla). Let's install Joomla! Copy the folder and paste "learnjoomla" folder to the **www** directory in **WAMP**. See the screenshot:

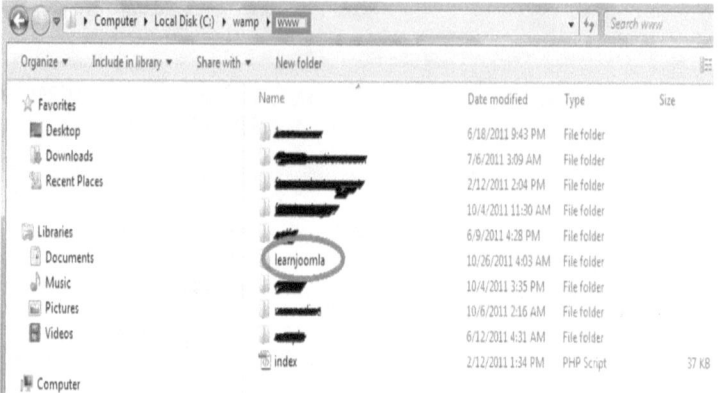

Now, you can access this folder from your web browser using the Path 'localhost/learnjoomla', so open your browser and type this address: 'localhost/learnjoomla' in it. You will be directed to the installation screen.

💡 You can also click on the WAMP serve icon on your taskbar and then click on 'localhost'. After that you will be directed to the WAMP server configuration page on your browser. There you can see your project (projects here means your website). Remember you created a folder 'learnjoomla'? Yes, that is your website.

The first step lets you select the language for installation. Just click **Next** and you will be shown a screen with all the settings of your web server and whether they are good for Joomla!, click **Next** at the top right of the page to proceed.

Chapter One - Obtaining and Installing Joomla!

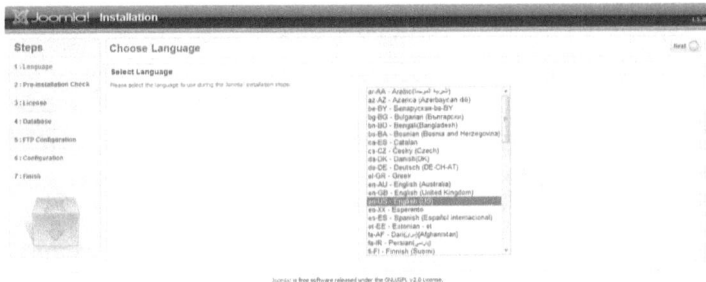

The second Step is the pre-installation check and **the third step** is just a license agreement that you have to agree by clicking Next. **The fourth step** is specifying the database settings.

Use the following settings

- ✓ Database Type : mysql

- ✓ Host Name : localhost

- ✓ Username : root

- ✓ Password: Leave it blank if you are using your local PC.

- ✓ Database Name: ljbase (I only used ljbase as an example; set your own database name.)

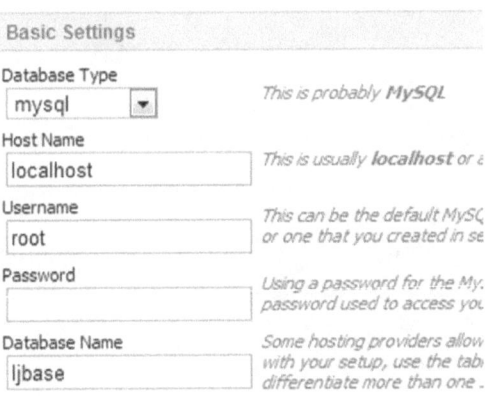

5

In this step, you provide the details of MySQL database to Joomla! and Joomla! will use this database to store all the content and other information. However, make sure you remember the database name you have created here; you will need it after you finish your website and have it ready to be uploaded to a host server.

Caution: You can only use the database name for only one project. Therefore, make a different database name for different project.—"advice".

The fifth step is to specify FTP setting to Joomla!, However, since we are installing Joomla! on a local computer, say NO to FTP and click Next. **The sixth step** is to specify the site name and a password for the administrator. You will have to fill the form with a name for the site, your e-mail address, and an administrator password. In this step, you have to click on the **"Install Sample Data"** button so that your website will initially have some sample data or content which you can edit or delete during your website restructure. After clicking on that button, you are shown a message **"Sample data installed successfully"**. Now click on Next to finish the installation.

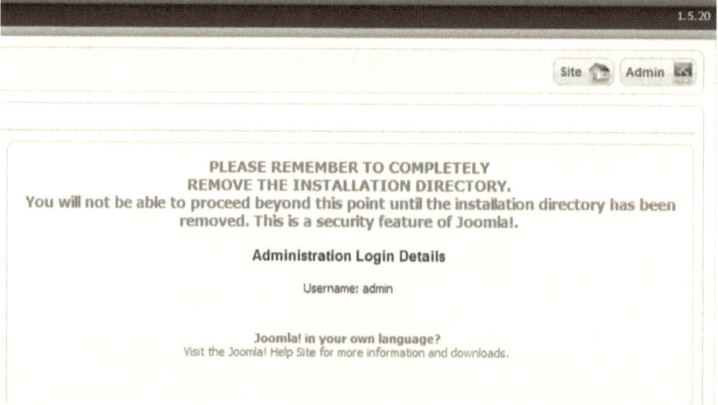

Before you can start using this Joomla! site, you have to delete the directory named **Installation** from the Joomla! folder. Deleting this folder serves as a security measure, just to make sure that nobody else reinstalls Joomla! using this folder. To remove the **Installation** folder,

Go to local Disk (C :) —> **wamp** —> **www** —> **learnjoomla**—> installation and hit delete.

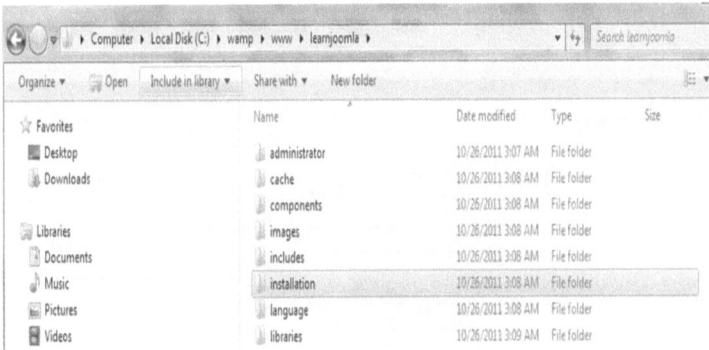

Congratulations! You have now successfully installed Joomla! 1.5 on your computer.

If you do not want to install the 'sample data', just click next to continue to final step. This means that at the end of the installation process, you will have a blank website and you need to build it from scratch. After the installation folder is deleted, you can either click on 'Site' to view the website or 'Admin' to redirect to the Back-end of the website where you continue your site restructure.

Exploring the Front—End

You have successfully installed Joomla! and you can access the website by typing the address 'localhost/learnjoomla' in your web browser. This is the default Joomla! site with the sample content. You will see how to modify this site according to your needs in the coming chapters. But at the moment, just feel free and navigate the site, clicking on different buttons and links trying them out. Try voting in the poll, and see the result instantly. You can also search for something using the search box. You can send a friend an article to his inbox or view the article in PDF format and you can also print it. Try it now!

💡 You can navigate the website in different ways and you get different content. This is a sample website and you can change any part of the content and layout to your satisfaction. Joomla! is just good to go.

- ✓ When you click on "More about Joomla!" you will be shown a list of categories, each having a short description. Selecting a category will show you a list of all the articles in that category. You may click on these to read the full articles.

- ✓ The poll is shown in a sidebar. When you vote in the poll, the results are shown in the main content area(we will talk more about poll in later chapter)

- ✓ When you click on Joomla! License "link" in the left menu, you will have a page displayed with the Joomla! License. This page is like a static page on a website.

- ✓ When you click on The News "link" in the main menu it will show introductions of different Articles, along with a "Read

More" link which shows the full article. This is similar to a blog because different articles are shown on the same page (we will discuss "Read More" in a later chapter.)

Joomla! Basics

As you might have known, Joomla! is a Content Management System software. In the simplest way, it means that it is used to manage contents of any type. However, to have a fully functional Joomla! website you must have a database.

- All Contents and images are all stored in the database.

- Whenever a guest visits the website, the front-end displays the contents stored in the database.

- The administrative back-end of Joomla! allows you to edit the content of the website or new content to it; you also can change the overall look of the website from the administrator back-end. It's considered as the workshop of your site.

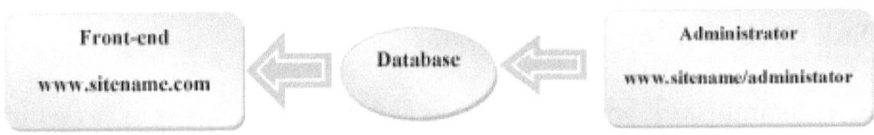

When you see Joomla! website, its front-end displays some of the content stored in the database. All the data used in the whole website development is stored in the database.

💡 The administrative interface lets you edit the database; hence you have the absolute control over the entire site.

Developing your First Website

At this point, we have successfully installed Joomla! 1.5 to our local PC; we are now going to develop a website. Let's move on.

Choose any name for your website, as for this book I am using my "My First Website" so now let's create a new website. However, we shall be creating a simple website with only five pages. This is how we do it;

> Setting the website name.

> Creating pages.

> Making the menu link to the created pages.

> Removing unwanted content from the website.

If you have installed the Joomla! 1.5 as described and shown earlier, then you can access your website by simply typing 'localhost/learnjoomla'; this will only show you the front-end of the site. For accessing the administrator interface of the website, you have to type 'localhost/learnjoomla/administrator' on your web browser.

Task ONE: Writing your Site Name

After login in with your username as "admin" and "password" as set in the installation process of Joomla!, you will be shown the admin panel. See the image below:

Chapter One - Obtaining and Installing Joomla!

- Click on the 'Global Configuration' button.

- You will be shown a different field which will let you specify the name of your website.

- At this point, use the "site name" field to write your website name. As stated above, we will use "**My First Website**" as the name of the site.

- After clicking on the Global configuration, you will be shown the next environment—GO to 'Site' and write the name of your website.

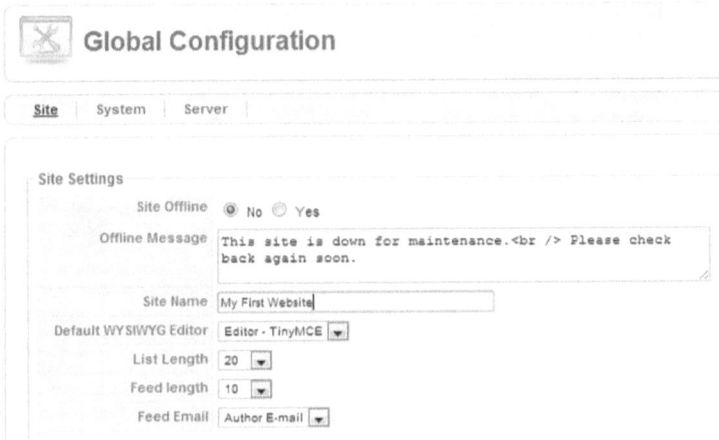

When you have written the name of the website, click on **Save**. The save button is at the top right of the admin page. You should get a message, "The global Configuration details have been updated".

Task TWO: Creating the Pages

As mentioned earlier, we are creating a simple website with just 5 pages. They are as follows:

1. HOME

2. ABOUT MY FIRST WEBSITE

11

3. WHY JOOMLA?

4. MORE ABOUT JOOMLA

5. WHATS NEW IN 1.5

It's very easy to create such pages. Just go to the back-end of your Joomla! site and click on the "Add New Article" button. You can also do this by going to ⟶Content⟶Article Manager in the menu and clicking on the New button.

- Type in the title for the page you are creating and write what you want in the content area of the page.

- In "Section" and "Category" choose both as uncategorized. Then click **Save** on the top right of the page.

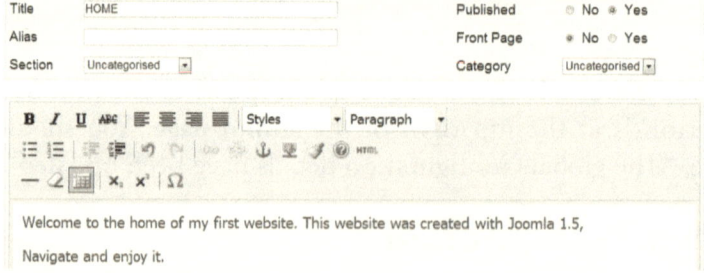

✎ We are not using the section and categories in this part. We shall discuss the Section and Categories in a later chapter.

- After saving the page, you will be redirected to the "Article Manager" where you can still edit the existing article, delete or create any new article.

Chapter One - Obtaining and Installing Joomla!

- Now click on the 'New button' on the top right in the "Article Manager" to create a new article page.

💡 When creating an article in your website, repeat the above step to keep creating pages. Do this process for the other four pages.

One good thing about this site is that Joomla! lets you write articles or pages using the reach text editor as shown in the screenshot below. This gives you the total control of how you want the look of your pages/articles to be, just the way you like it!. The text editor is like the Microsoft Word processing software. You can insert images, links, emoticons, and many more features.

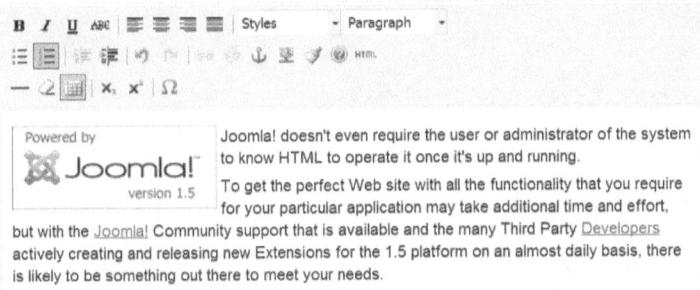

Now that we have created all the five pages using the same process, let's move on to the next Task which is creating menu link to those pages.

Caution: The pages will not be visible in the front-end until we link it to menu and get them published.

Task THREE: Making the Menu link to the created pages

Joomla! website has different menus. The menus are in Modules and Modules can be set to different position within the site. This is based on how you want your site to look like; you have absolute control over the look of the website. Now menus can be linked to the newly created pages and those links will be displayed on the website when a visitor clicks on the menu link. See the next image:

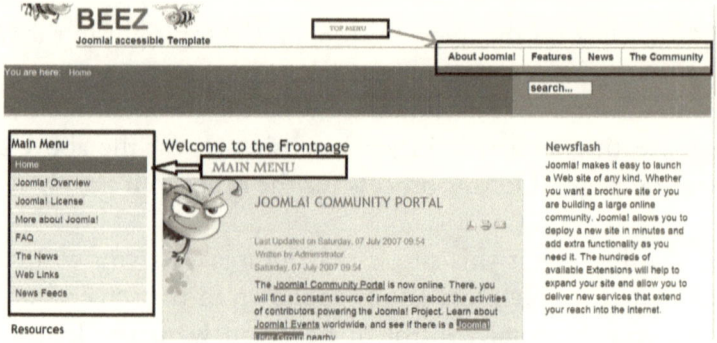

To view all the list of the menus on the main menu you have to Go Admin panel ⟶Menus ⟶main menu.

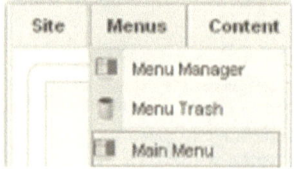

After clicking on the Main Menu, you now have to click on the **New** button (this is on the top right) to create a new menu link for one of the pages created earlier in the Article Manager. You will be shown a list of menu item types, but for now:

- Click on the 'article' why? Because we want the new menu to be linked to one of the articles we have created earlier.

- Click on "article layout". This means that when the Menu is clicked, the selected article will display on the site in a single page layout.

Chapter One - Obtaining and Installing Joomla!

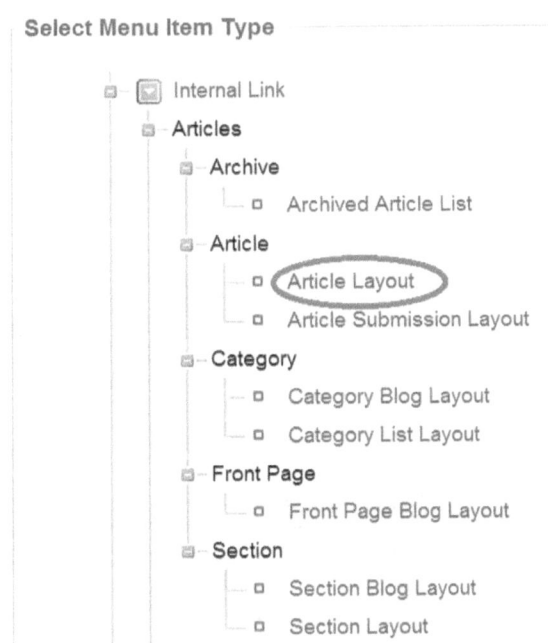

- Next is the page where you specify the Title of the menu link and the article you want to be shown when it is clicked in the front-end.

- After that, at the top right of the same page; you will see the **Parameter (Basic)**. You will have to click on the "**select**" button to select the article you want to link to the menu.

When the menu link is clicked on the site, the article selected here will be displayed.

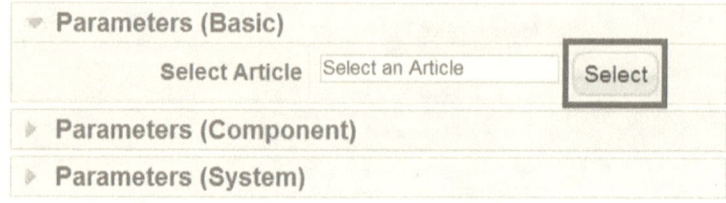

You will then get a pop-up window to select from the number of articles. We have created five pages of article and we will select the 'HOME' article because we want people to see the home page when they click on the HOME link in the Main Menu.

- Now, **select** HOME as seen in the image below:

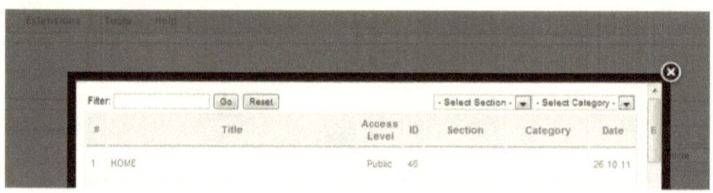

- After selecting the article, the 'select article' field will show the article you have selected which is "HOME" in this case.

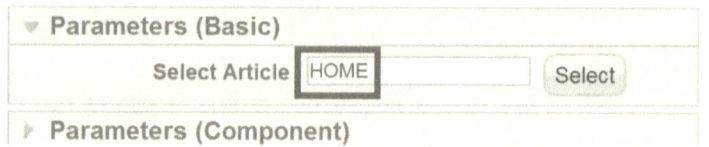

- Now that you have done all of this, you will have to click the **Save** button. This is at the top right of the same page.

Caution: Make sure you save all work before leaving the page. If you leave the page without saving, the changes done will not be applied on your website.

When we install the Joomla! Sample data website, there is a "Home" link in the main menu by default. At this point if you refresh you site (front-end), you will notice there will be TWO "Home" links in the main menu—'Home' and 'HOME' (the one you just created is

Chapter One - Obtaining and Installing Joomla!

the one with the Capital letters). This action is to show you how to create a menu link to your site. See the screenshot to notice the menu changes.

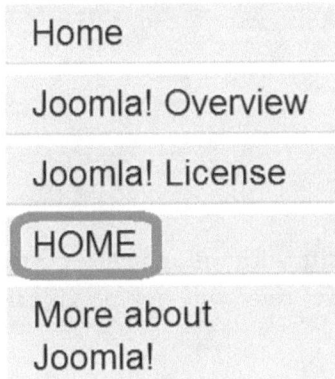

All you need to do now is to repeat the 'same steps' to create menu links for the remaining four articles that you created earlier. You will link each article to the new menu you create. Just follow the steps above.

💡 You can write any name in the new menu. The menu title is what will be displayed on the main menu and not the article title. Once clicked, the article content will be shown on the website content page.

You have now created five pages ready with some contents in them and the menu links connecting them. However, now we need:

- All other Modules to be discarded in the front-end; this will allow us to have contents related to "learnjoomla" i.e., the Main Menu in which we have five menus in.

- When the site is visited through 'localhost/learnjoomla', the HOME page that you created will be shown. This is simply because it is set as the default homepage. To make "HOME" the Default page, select the HOME link in the Main Menu Manager and click on the Yellow Star icon.

- All other links visible in the Menus are to be removed.

17

See the next screenshot to understand better.

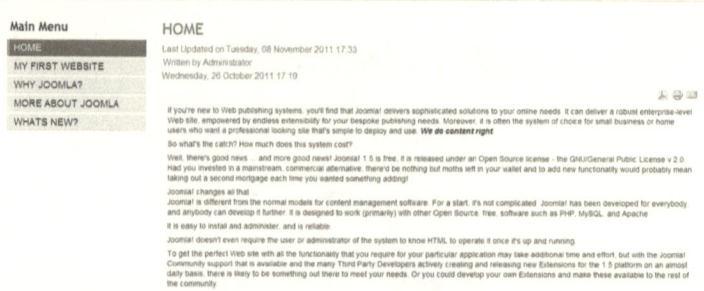

The image shows the site with only the five created menus; other menus are disabled. Therefore, they will not be visible on the website front-end.

You are using the sample data which already have lots of menus and content created by Joomla!. But in this situation, you have to clean up all unwanted or irrelevant menus and Modules in the site to get the desired result.

IMPORTANT If you are familiar with Joomla!, during the installation process "do not" install the sample data. Just make a normal installation as this will give you the chance to build your site from scratch without any predefined menus or articles. I used the sample data site to give you a better picture on how the whole Joomla! website will look like when you finish building it. You have absolute control of the site and you can design it to your taste (depending on the kind of website you are developing).

The next image shows the front-end with the messy page Joomla! generates. When the sample data is installed, you will have those menus. However, you will see that it has too many things in it; these "things" are called 'Modules' and we show them in red boxes in the following picture. The only Module needed now is the "Main Menu" module. Therefore, all other Modules are not needed by our "learnjoomla" website.

Chapter One - Obtaining and Installing Joomla!

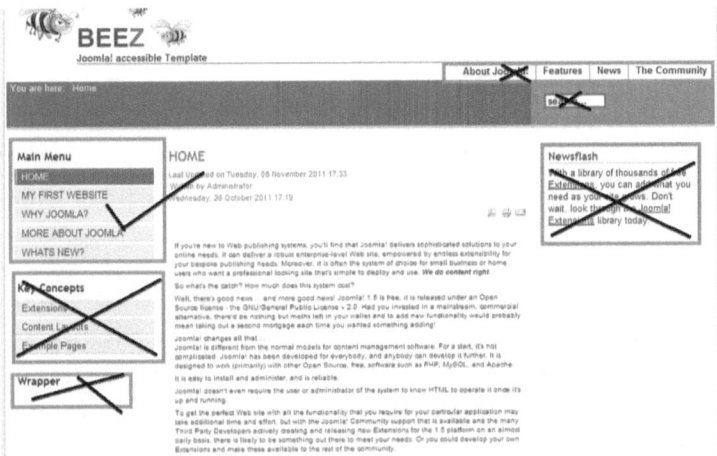

To hide those unnecessary Modules showing on the page, go to the administrator back-end of the site by pointing the browser to "localhost/learnjoomla/administrator" and login. Now go to Extensions → Module Manager using the menu. The Module Manager lets you manage all the Modules. Here, you will see a list of all the currently installed Modules on the site, (you get all this Modules on display only because you installed the sample data during the installation process). There may be about 24 items in the list.

Now tick the check boxes at the left of each Module name to select all of them except for "Main Menu", and then click on the "Disable" button at the top right. Doing this will hide all those Modules.

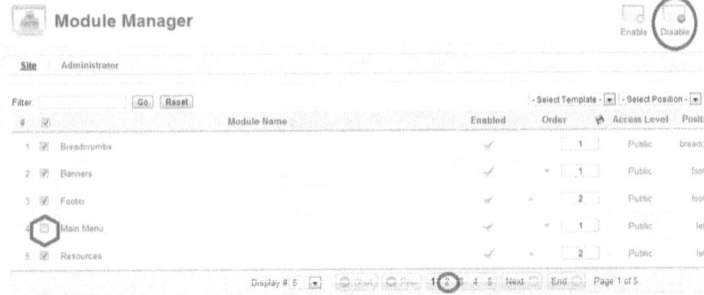

The List of Modules may extend to 2,3,4, or more pages, so you will have to go to the next page by clicking '2,3,4, or any page' at the

19

bottom of the list. Then disable the Modules from the second page too following the same check list process. You can also decide to show all the Modules by simply selecting the "All" option below the Module Manager "Display #".

Caution: Do not check and disable the Main Menu. It is the menu we wish to display on the website.

To clean up all the mess in the site front-end which is not required, we will hide all links other than the ones linked to the five pages created earlier. Then we will make the "HOME" page that we created as the default page to be shown when you see the website; i.e., when a visitor opens the site, the first page that displays will be the "HOME" page.

- To do this, simply Go to the back-end and open the Menu Manager. For Main Menu, go to Menus ⟶ Main Menu. You will be shown a list of all the links currently seen in the Main Menu.

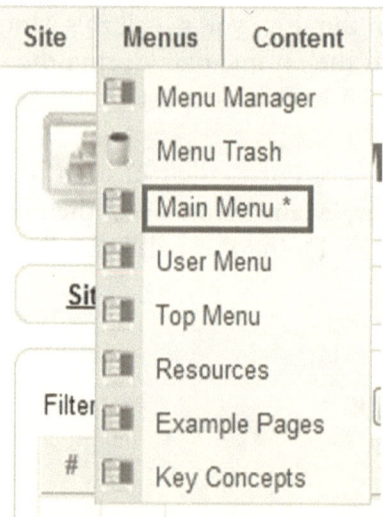

- To make the HOME page default, select it using the checkbox and click on the "Default" button on the top right (its yellow in color with the star like shape). Now, you will note that a small star appears next to this link item. Make the Home link

Chapter One - Obtaining and Installing Joomla!

you created earlier as the "HOME" default. In this case, the home link is in capital letters.

If you decide not to show some of the menu links on your site, it's simple; just do like you did for other Modules by selecting all the menus in which are not required. Then simply click on "Unpublish". In other words, select all the links except for the ones you created before, i.e., five pages and then click on the "Unpublish" button at the top right of the Menu manager page.

The "Publish" button when clicked on an article, menu, Module or any component means that that item will be displayed or rather be visible in the site front-end. "Unpublish" simply means that items selected will not be in use or visible within the site until set otherwise.

The five-page site we created will have the look identical to the following picture: you can edit, add or delete any content of the website. To do this, simply login to the administrator panel (back-end) and go to article Manager to select items to edit, delete or even add new article. It looks beautiful and yet it's a simple five—page website. Joomla! can do even better!

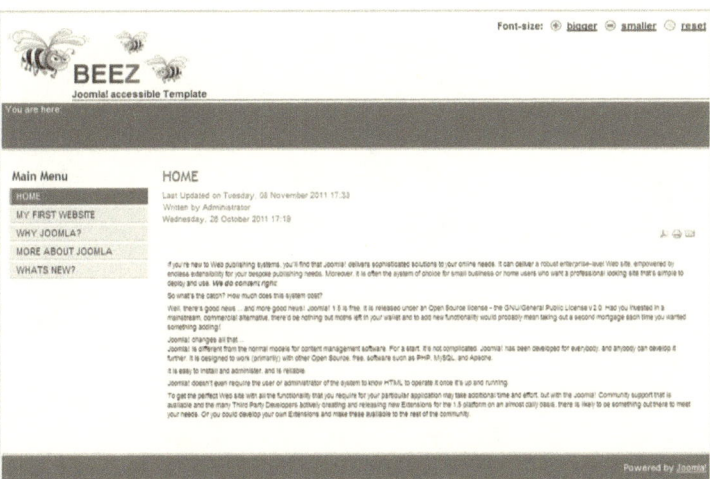

When you carefully read the steps above and apply it in the development of your website, the best result is assured as Joomla! is a great software that makes it all easy for you to design and develop your website in just minutes. The best part is that, "You do not need any technical skills to develop your website using Joomla! and it's absolutely free." You can download Joomla! 1.5 in the official Joomla! website at www.joomla.org

Installing Joomla! is probably the biggest problem in getting started on creating your website. However, you will need to get a WAMP server installed and of course the Joomla! 1.5 Package. Once you have these two steps complete, it's very easy for you to use Joomla! to build and develop your website.

Chapter Two

Creating Contents and Menus

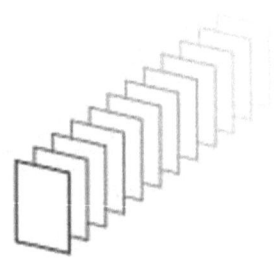

One of the most important parts of a website is the content. However in Joomla!, an Article is a piece of content consisting of text (HTML), possibly with links to other resources. For example, images, links and so on can be within an article. Each article you have represents a category and a category can be in other categories. You can also have an "uncategorized" article which means it exists alone and doesn't associate with any category. Yet this will be displayed on your website. These articles are maintained using the article manager in the back-end of the Joomla! administrator panel.

Adding Content to the Front Page

You will be shown how to add an article to the front page of your website. To do this:

1. Login to the Administrator back-end.

2. Click on the "Add New Article" button in the main Control Panel to open the New Article screen or,

   Click the Content→Article Manager→New Article menu item to go to the Article Manager. Then click the new toolbar button.

After clicking on the new article, you will be taken to the new article screen which contains options for categorizing and naming the article, editing content and selecting parameters. In this case, just select the uncategorized.

3. Enter a title in the Title field. This is used when the article title is displayed.

4. Enter an alias in the Alias field. By default Joomla! will create the alias for the title you have set. The alias helps in search engine optimization.

5. Select a Category using the drop down menus. As mentioned earlier, choose the uncategorized since we're not setting the article to a category now.

6. Choose whether the article is to be published or not using the Published drop down menu.

7. Choose whether the article will be displayed on the home page using the Featured drop down menu.

8. Now enter your content using the editor in the New Article screen.

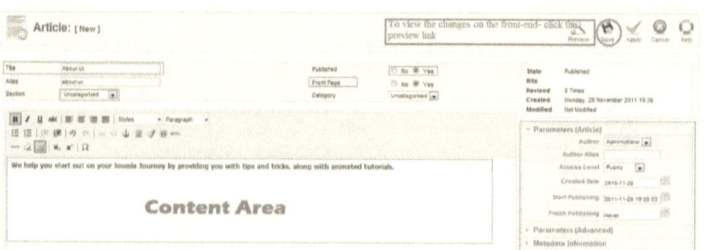

9. You may also choose Parameters for the article. Click on each section to view the parameters and change the settings to suit your requirements.

10. Click the **Save** toolbar button to save your article.

You will see the article you just created in the front page when you preview it; it will appear like the following image.

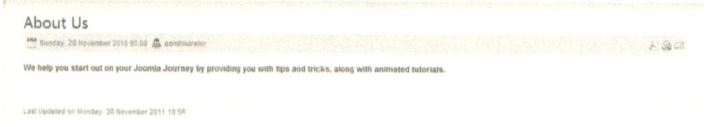

You have successfully created an article and displayed it in the front-end of your site. However, you might want to create other articles but you don't want them to be displayed on the front-end. It's simple; set it to NO in the front page option on the article page.

- The **Save** toolbar button will save your changes and return you to the Article Manager screen.

- The **Apply** button will save your changes but will leave you in the Article Edit screen.

- You can edit the article anytime and as much as you want. Just click on the article title in the article manger and edit it.

- You have to complete the Article Title, Section or Category fields, or else you will see an error message.

Using the 'Read More' in an article

Sometimes you have an article that is too large to display on the front page of your website; you probably want people to read all the articles but then only some parts can be shown on the front page. This serves as an introduction (intro) of the article. Joomla! has a special feature called, "Read More" which allows you to read other parts of the article. To do this lets add a new article:

1. Follow the steps in the "Adding Content to the Front Page" above. Go to Article Manager and select any of the articles which you want to add the read more link to. Alternatively you might choose to edit an existing article to add the feature. It is allowed in Joomla!

2. Now point your cursor to any place within the article content.

3. Scroll down to the bottom of the page and click the Read More button.

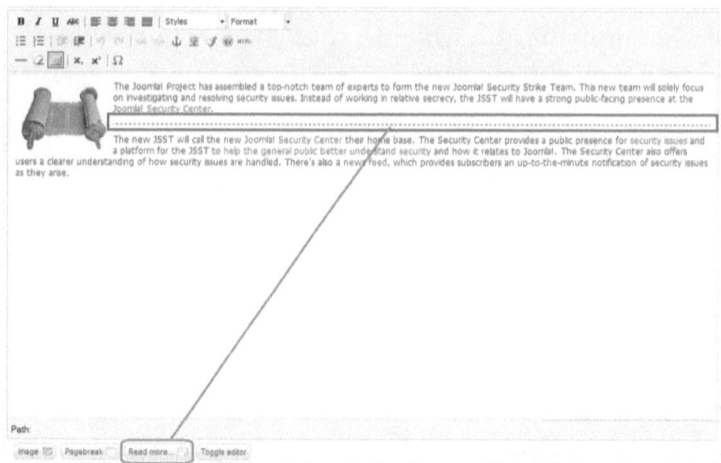

4. Now click **Apply** to see the changes in the front-end, and if you are satisfied click Save on the top right of the Page.

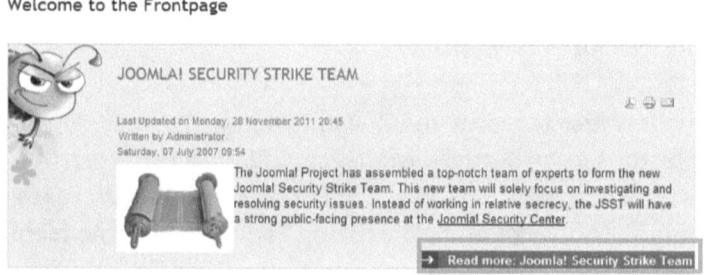

You should see the above result on your site front page. To read the full article, click on the Read more link.

The Apply button allows you to save your changes and still remain on the article edit page, but when you hit the **Save** button, it saves the changes and redirect you to the Article Manager.

MENU

You will not have a good website unless there's a menu to help users navigate to different pages. Joomla! has a built-in system for managing menus. This system is built around the three types of information in Joomla!:

- Components

- Modules

- Plugins

Components are the main information in Joomla! and are driven by menus. If you look at the front page of your site, you can see only the front page articles. The contact information, web links, news feeds, and articles not published on the front page are not visible. This is because each page displays one component at a time.

1. Go to your (back-end) http://localhost/learnjoomla/administrator and login with the username "admin" and password you specified during the installation.

2. From the "Menus", select "Main Menu".

If you are already logged in, you do not need to do this again.

Home Page

The default menu in Joomla! is the "Home" link, it provides access to articles which you have enabled in the "Front Page" option. You can click on "Home" to edit many of its settings including the name of the home page as well as the number of articles that are displayed.

3. Click on "Home" to configure the home page.

4. In the "**Parameters(Basic)**" area, there are a number of different options you can configure:

    - **#Leading** is the number of article intros to display on the front page with a "read more" link to see the entire article. These articles will stretch the entire width of the news box.

- **#Intro** is the number of article intros to display on the front page with a "read more" link to see the entire article. These articles will fill only the width of one column, not the entire page.

- **#Columns** is the number of columns in which articles are displayed.

- **#Links** is the number of articles to display only as links at the bottom of the page.

5. In **Parameters (Advanced),** make sure that "Show a Feed Link" is set to **YES**. This will make the front page accessible by an RSS news feed.

6. In **Parameters (System),** enter a title for the page inside of the "Page Title" field. This will display in the browser's header as well as in the header for that page in the document.

7. Click **Save** to finish setting up the home page.

Changing the Default menu item

When people first check your site, you may want to show them a specific page on your website, and that page that you show them is called the default page. This, however, means that whenever someone goes to your website, the first thing he sees is the default page that you set. Instead of using Joomla! we will reset the default page to another menu item. To do this, simply:

1. Go to Menus⟶ Main Menu.

2. By default, "Home" is set to the default.

3. Select any other menu item and click the Yellow star button located at the top middle of the page.

You can change the default page as many times as you wish but you cannot assign a default page to more than one Menu item at the same time.

Creating Individual Pages of Content

When you are building a website, you usually build menu links for specific pages and Joomla! has a great menu system where you can add links to individual article. However, you will learn how to link articles to menus. You have learned how to create an article earlier in this chapter; repeat the same step to create as many articles as you wish. In the process of creating the new article, remember not to set the article to show on the "front page" and select "uncategorized" for the section. Set the article as "Publish" so that when you create the menu link your article will be displayed if the menu is clicked in the front-end.

You have created the Article, now do the following:

1. Go to Menus⟶Main Menu and click add New.

    You will notice a list of menus you can choose from.

2. Select "Article". This gives different options that deals with articles displays, but we only want to show article that displays one at a time.

3. Select "Article layout".

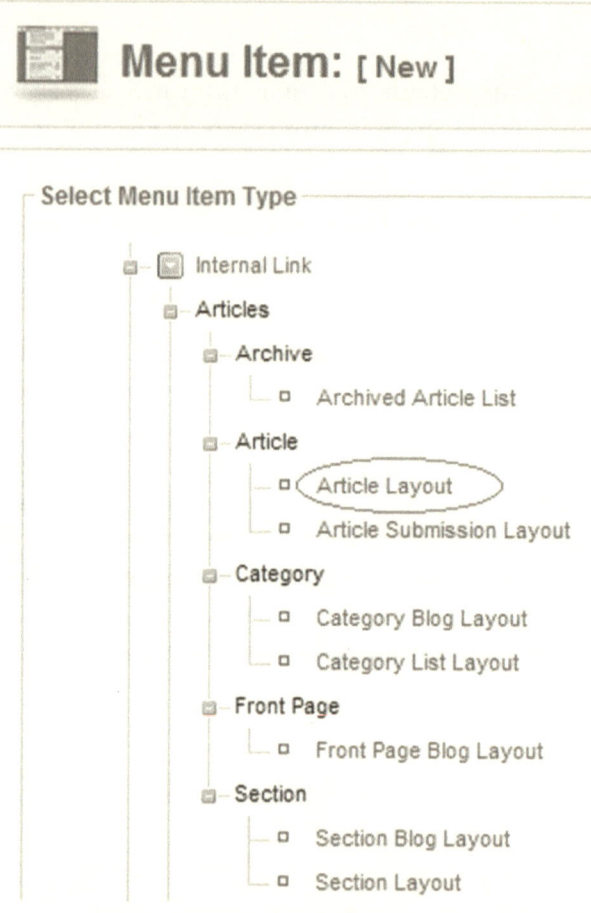

4. You will now be shown a page where you create your menu link.

Chapter Two - Creating Contents and Menus

5. Write the title of the menu link you want to show on the main menu.

6. Select the article you want to link to the menu.

7. Click **Save**.

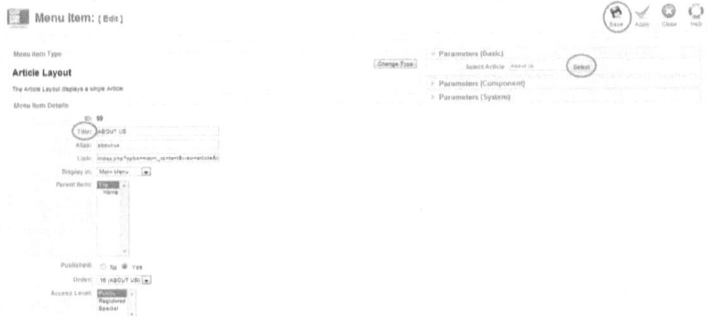

8. Preview the site on the top right of the back-end page.

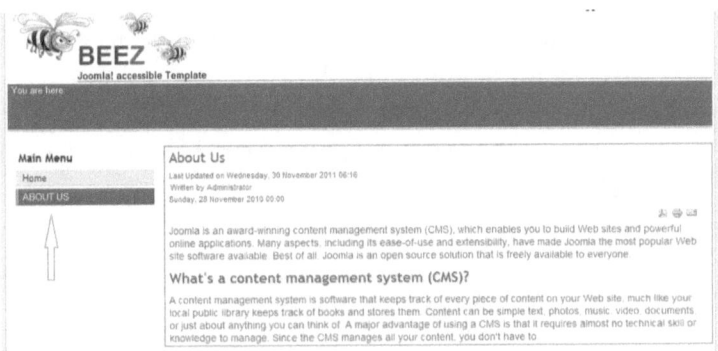

You have successfully created an "ABOUT US" menu link to the front-end of your site under the main menu. When a user clicks on the "ABOUT US" menu, it displays the article linked to it.

Tips: You can add as many Menu links as you wish, simply repeat the steps shown above.

Ak Shehu

Creating Parent Menu Items

When you are building your website, sometimes you have a group of links that you only want to show after another item is clicked; Joomla! helps you manage these types of groupings. To start:

1. Go to the Menus⟶Main Menu.

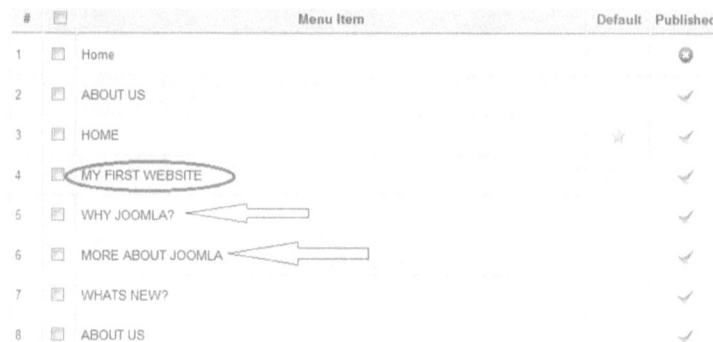

We want to make Number 4 (item) the Father of 5 & 6.

2. Click on the item you want to be a child to another (here we click on 5) and you will be taken to a new page.

3. Go to the Parent items and select the Father (i.e. item 4 "MY FIRST WEBSITE").

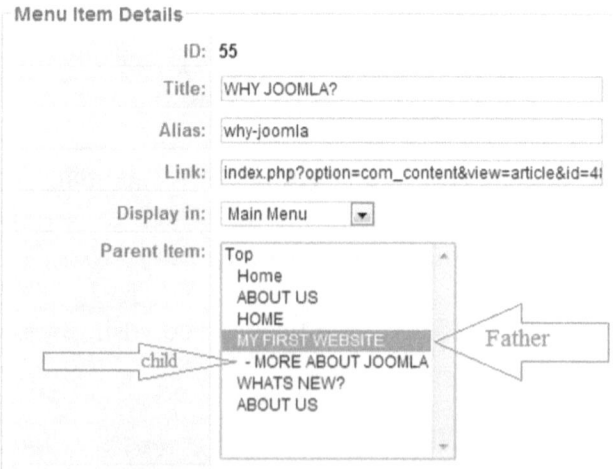

Chapter Two - Creating Contents and Menus

4. Click **Save** and you will be redirected to "Menu item Manager".

5. Go to the front-end of your site and see the changes. When you click on the Father, it shows a list of children.

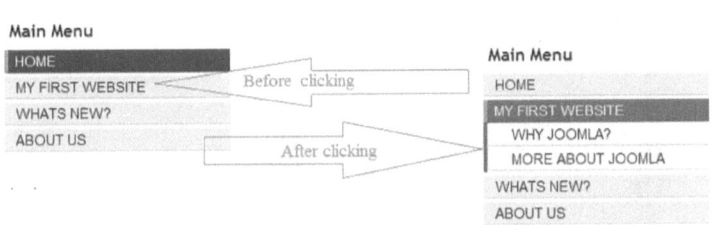

Dividing long article using the page breaks

Dividing long articles into sections is a helpful way of presenting content. Joomla! can be used to divide long articles into multiple pages which are linked using 'Previous and Next' page navigation and also a Table of Contents section which is displayed as part of the article. To divide a long Article into multiple linked pages:

1. Open the Article for editing using either of the two procedures:

    - Click Content→Article Manager menu item to go to the Article Manager, select the Article and click the Edit toolbar button.

    - Clicking the "Add New Article" button in the Control Panel.

2. If logged in to the Front-end, you have appropriate permissions and are viewing the Article you wish to edit: Click the Edit toolbar button.

3. Locate the position in the content where the first page should end with the cursor.

35

4. Click the Pagebreak editor button at the bottom of the page.

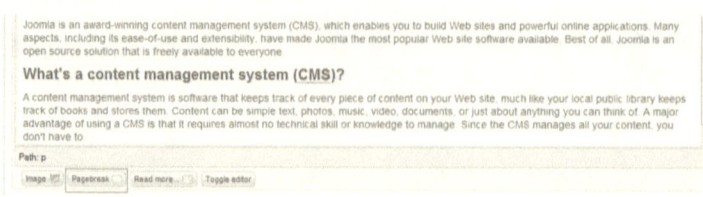

5. The Insert Pagebreak screen will open as shown in the next image.

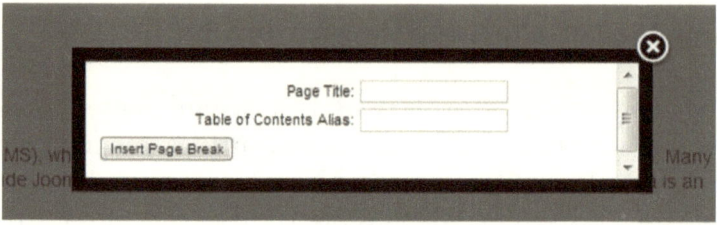

6. Enter the Page Title and Table of Contents Alias as required:

7. **Page Title:** Allows you to enter a sub title for the page displayed after the Article title. If left blank the main Article title will be used.

8. **Table of Contents Alias:** Used to give a shortened name for the Table of Contents which is displayed as part of multiple page Articles. If left blank the link will be displayed as Page #.

9. Click the **Insert Pagebreak** button. The screen will close and a horizontal rule will be inserted to show the location of the Pagebreak.

10. To close the Insert Pagebreak screen without inserting a Pagebreak, click the **X** close button.

➤ To remove a Pagebreak, delete the horizontal rule using the delete or backspace keys.

Caution: It is not possible to edit the Page Title and Table of Contents Alias using the content editor once it has been inserted. To modify the Pagebreak you can do one of the following:

- Delete and re-insert the pagebreak using the process described above, or;

- Edit the raw HTML of the Article using the editor and modify the title and alt attributes of the relevant <hr→ HTML tag.

Formatting content and adding external link

Plain text can be boring. Joomla! uses What You See Is What You Get (WYSIWYG) Editor that works a bit like Microsoft Word. You might want to add and change some of the article looks. You can do this by selecting your article in the Article Manager or simply create new article. You have already created an article. So simply do the following:

1. Go to Article Manager and select the article you want to format.

2. In the content area you will notice on the editor you have something like Bold (B) italic (I) underline (u) and so on.

Now let's put a bullet point for some of our content list and insert an external link.

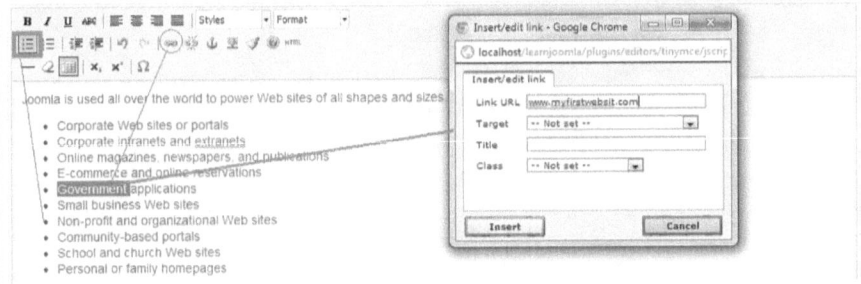

1. To make the point a bullet points, highlight the content and click on the "unordered list" on the editor.

2. To insert a link, highlight the word you want to link to another website and click the link icon on the editor.

3. You get a pop up, type in all details including the URL address and click insert.

4. Now after editing your content. Click on **Apply** button on the top right of the page to see changes on your site. If you are satisfied.

5. Click **Save**.

Adding Article images

A picture is worth a thousand words and your website is not an exception. Joomla! has a built in image browser you can use to add images to your articles. We, however, will upload an image to the site and then add it to the article. Let's make it happen now.

1. Create a new article by going to the Article Manager and add new or if you want to use an existing article.

2. Go to Article manager and select an article by clicking on the article.

3. After opening the content area of your article, it's time to upload the image from your computer to the website before adding the image to the article.

4. Upload Using Media Manager. The simplest way to add images is to upload them from your computer using the Media Manager.

- You have to download the image onto your computer and be able to find it, it is even better if you have the suitable image on your computer already.

- Then, from the Control Panel (back-end interface) navigate to Site⟶Media Manager.

5. Pick a subdirectory where you want the image to be located; you can also create a new folder for your Images.

6. At the bottom of the page is an Upload box. Click **Choose file** to locate the image on your computer, then "Upload" to upload the file to the server.

💡 Always upload your images under the stories folder. But I would advise you creating a new sub-folder under Stories folder.

Caution: You cannot insert an image to the article direct from your computer; you must have the image in your Media Manger of the Joomla! back-end.

Now that you have uploaded an image to the media manager, let's insert an image to the Article. To do this:

1. Open the Article you want to insert an image in.

2. Navigate your cursor to the point you wish to insert the image in the content area.

3. Click the "Image" button at the bottom of the page; you will get a popup.

4. Select the image you wish from the "*stories folder*" or a subfolder you created.

5. Write a description, title and check the caption if you want the image to have a caption.

6. **Align**: Select the alignment position of the image: left or Right. You may also not choose any.

7. Click "Insert" on the top right of the popup.

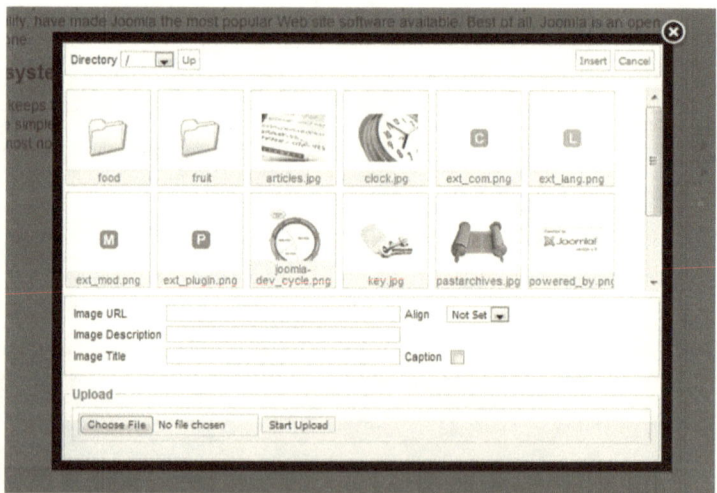

You can also use the popup to upload an image in the directory. Then click the image button at the bottom of the article page to insert the image to the article.

💡 It's always nice to set the Alignment of the image as it makes the content look very professional. However, this also depends on where you wish to place the image within the article.

Ordering Articles

There are times when you will want to order articles on your website. For example you have Article (A) & Article (B) on your FrontPage. Now you want A to be down and B to be on top. This is how you do it

1. Go to the Article Manager.

2. Use the green arrows to push down the article or push up the article; and you are done.

3. Go to the FrontPage and view the changes. You will notice that the article you pushed down will be displayed below the other one. It depends on how you will like your orderings. See the image below:

You may also use the number to set the ordering, but remember to click **Save** at the top on the numbering.

Deleting Contents

There are times which you want to delete some content on your site, Joomla! allows you to delete content easily. When you delete an article, it goes to "Trash". However, that article will no longer be visible on your website. Remember, when you delete an article it goes to "Trash". To delete it permanently:

1. Go to the Article Trash under the Content in the back-end of your Joomla site!

2. Select the article you wish to delete permanently and click, "Delete". It will now be deleted permanently on your website.

To restore an earlier trashed article, do the same step but now click on the "Restore" button. Joomla! will restore back your article to the article manager and your article will not be **Published**. This is to make sure that you don't publish articles you don't want to show on your site. However to publish it, check the **Red Cross** on the article to **Green tick** and the article is back to published and can be visible on your website.

Setting Global Configuration Parameters for Articles

Joomla! provides a control panel to help set the parameter of the entire article that will be created in your website. To do this simply:

1. Go to the Article Manager.

2. Click on parameters on the top right of the page.

3. Make all necessary changes and click **Save**.

✎ Joomla! has made basic settings for you by default. Leave the Global Configuration parameters for articles as it is, and it's better to make your changes in the individual article parameters.

Setting Individual Article Configuration Parameters

Parameters (Article)

These entries are optional. However, Joomla! automatically creates default entries for these values.

- **Author.** Select the Author from the drop-down list box. Default is the current user.

- **Author Alias.** This optional field allows you to enter in an alias for this Author for this Article. This allows you to display a different Author name for this Article.

- **Access Level.** Who has access to this item? Current options are:

- ✓ Public: Everyone has access.

- ✓ Registered: Only registered users have access.

- ✓ Special: Only users with author status or higher have access. You can change an item's Access Level by clicking on the icon in the column.

- **Created Date.** This field defaults to the current time when the Article was created. You can enter in a different date and time or click on the calendar icon to find the desired date.

- **Start Publishing.** Date and time to start publishing. Use this field if you want to enter content ahead of time and then have it published automatically at a future time.

- **Finish Publishing.** Date and time to finish publishing. Use this field if you want to have content automatically changed to unpublished state at a future time (example, when it is no longer applicable).

Parameters (Advanced)

This section allows you to enter additional parameters for this Article. These parameters allow you to override the parameters set in the Parameter/Global Configuration setup in the Article Manager and the Parameters-Component settings in the Menu Item Manager.

A value of 'Use Global' means that either the setting from the Menu Item or the setting from the Global Configuration will control the action. A setting other than 'Use Global' will always control the action and override settings from these other areas. The setting here takes top priority. The setting in the Menu Item is second priority. The setting in the Global Configuration controls if both of the other setting are set to 'Use Global'. See the next image:

Parameters (Advanced)

Show Title	Use Global
Title Linkable	Use Global
Intro Text	Use Global
Section Name	Use Global
Section Title Linkable	Use Global
Category Title	Use Global
Category Title Linkable	Use Global
Article Rating	Use Global
Author Name	Use Global
Created Date and Time	Use Global
Modified Date and Time	Use Global
PDF Icon	Use Global
Print Icon	Use Global
E-mail Icon	Use Global
Content Language	- Select Language -
Key Reference	
Alternative *Read more:*	

Metadata Information

Metadata is information about the Article that is not displayed but is available to Search Engines and other systems to classify the Article. This gives you more control over how the content will be analyzed by these programs. All of these entries are optional. The next image shows where you can put the entries.

![Metadata Information form with Description, Keywords, Robots, and Author fields]

- **Metadata Description.** Optional Metadata Description for this Article.

- **Metadata Keywords.** Optional entry for keywords; must be entered separated by commas (for example, "cow, bag, and dog") and may be entered in upper or lower case. (For example, "BAGS" will match "bag" or "Bags"). Keywords can be used in several ways. You can get more details on metadata from your host provider or SEO professionals as this is beyond the scope of this book.

Toolbar

These are key tools often used in Joomla! Back-end.

Preview: This opens a popup window that displays a preview of the Article. This is normally not needed when using a WYSIWYG editor, such as TinyMCE, Artof Editor and so on.

Save: It saves it and return to editing the menu details, either article manager, menu manager etc.

Apply: This saves your work, but let's you stay in the same screen. If you have been working on a screen for a long time and don't want to risk losing your work, pressing **Apply** saves your work and lets you continue working. If, for example, you lost your internet connection, your work will be saved up to this point.

Close: This returns you to the previous screen without saving your work. If you press 'Close' while adding a new item, this new item will not be created. If you were modifying an existing item, the modifications will not be saved.

Help: This opens the 'Help' screen which provides you with more information about a particular issue.

Chapter Three

Understanding Sections and Categories

This chapter will provide you with an overview of how Sections, Categories and Articles are all perfected in Joomla! to make a good Website. Joomla! can do much better than only Contents Management system. It is, however, important to potential Joomla! Website Developers to at least have the basic understanding of how Joomla! is actually set up to organize content. Note that proper content organization can significantly improve the flow and usability of your website. Generally, Joomla! uses a logical approach to manage the website structure and present website content to the visitor of the site. The following image demonstrates the basic concept for how sections, categories, articles and menu items relate to each other to form a logical structure to enable you to manage your website and for visitors to locate information more efficiently.

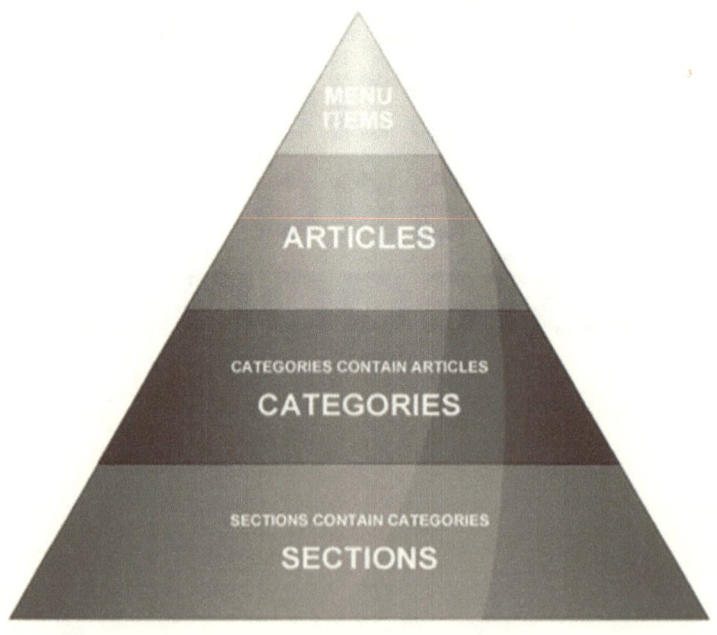

Sections

Sections are used to manage or structure your categories in a logical order. You cannot create a category without first creating a section to store the category in. You are not limited to just one section, and depending on how complex your Joomla! website is you may wish to create a number of sections in order to structure your site.

Categories

Categories are used to store and manage articles. Each category must be associated with a section. You are not limited to just creating one category you can create different categories and associate them with a specific section.

Articles

Articles are stored in categories or they can be outside a category using the "uncategorized" feature in the section of the article pages. However, Articles can only be associated with one category and not multiple categories.

Menu items

Menu items are designed to help visitors navigate to specific articles, categories or sections. When you create a menu item you can link directly to a section, category or uncategorized article. The Menu items are not just limited to linking to sections, categories or uncategorized articles. You can create a menu item to link to a third-party component or the built-in components like contacts, poll, search and many more.

Before beginning, I strongly suggest you to login to the Administrator panel of your website and visit Section, Category Manager Pages for a few minutes and try to understand how sections and categories are used in real time. However, if you will publish lots of articles in your website, you should create sections, categories and then put articles under proper category. However, if you plan to build a website which will have only a few pages, you don't need to create sections and categories. You can set articles as "uncategorized" (which means that it doesn't belong to a section or category) and link to these articles from main menu, but if you decide to publish your content under categories and will not use sections, you should again create a section first and put categories under that section.

Content Structure of Joomla!

Joomla! was basically designed to organize content in Section⟶ Category⟶Content item structure take a look at a basic structure of the contents in Joomla!:

- NEWS (Section)

    ✓ America(Category)

    ✓ Asia(Category)

    - Sports Asia⟶ (Article)

    - Talk Asia⟶ (Article)

    ✓ Africa(Category)

    ✓ Europe(Category)

The above structure simply means that NEWS is a Section that contains America and Asia as Categories. Sports Asia and Talk Asia are both Articles in the Asia Category. I hope you get the scope; it's important to get the idea before moving on to develop the structure of your website. It is also advisable to know what kind of website you want to develop as it will help you in the structuring.

Must Know-About Content Structuring in Joomla!

1. You should really know what your site is about before you create your first section or category. Many people get so confused that they can just enter content as easily as they create documents in a word processor that they lose site of the fact that the site should have a purpose. You should have a goal. Your content structure should show the overall purpose of your site.

2. Design your Structure on Paper

Avoid creating Sections and Categories as soon as you have successfully installed Joomla!. You will be glad you did months from now when you realize that you created a category out of a topic that should really be a section. This is relatively easy to fix, but why not just do it right the first time? It helps a lot.

You should create a hierarchy of major topics and sub-topics. Soon, you will start to see the organization of your site take shape. Once you are satisfied that you have your structure designed, then you can start creating Sections and Categories. Now do the next Step

3. Create your Sections

The top level in the Joomla! content structure is called a "Section". Sections are used to differentiate between groups of content Categories. Now that you have all of your Sections and Categories defined on paper, it is time to start creating Sections in your Joomla! back-end. To Create Sections, Do these steps in every section that you want to create in Joomla!:

- ✓ Login to your Joomla! Administrator control panel (Back-end).

- ✓ Click on Content⟶Section Manager.

- ✓ In the Section Manager, click New in the toolbar.

- ✓ Fill in the necessary information. The only thing you need is a Title. The other fields are optional.

- ✓ Click **Save** in the toolbar.

4. To Create Category

The second level in the Joomla! content structure is called a "Category". Categories are used to differentiate between groups of content items. Now that all of your Sections are in place, you can start adding Categories. Do these steps in every section that you want to create in Joomla!:

- ✓ Log in to your administrator control panel.

- ✓ Click on Content⟶Category Manager.

- ✓ In the Category Manager, click New in the toolbar.

- ✓ Fill in the necessary information. The only thing you need is a Title. The other fields are optional.

- ✓ Click **Save** in the toolbar.

5. Time to add your Content

At this point, you're ready to start adding content in Joomla! Just remember to fit in content item in the correct Section/Category.

Uncategorized contents are also known as Static content; these are basically just uncategorized content items. You should have few static content items in your site. Any content item that you have that does not fit into one of your pre-defined categories should be a static (uncategorized) content item. Example could be the "**About us page**" of any company website. It's not necessary to be under a section or category.

Chapter Three - Understanding Sections and Categories

Why Use Sections and Categories?

There are two main reasons you might want to organize your Articles in sections and categories. These are List and Blog Layouts.

In Joomla! there are built-in Menu Item Types that take advantage of this organization. These are the Section Blog, Section List, Category Blog, and Category List. These Menu Item Types (are also called "layouts") make it very easy to show articles that belong to sections or categories. See the next image:

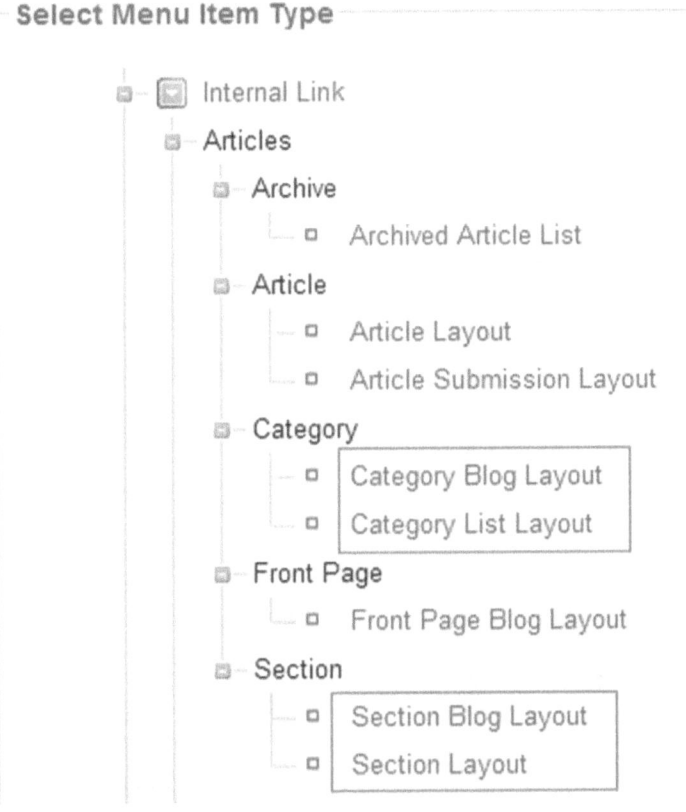

As new articles are created and assigned to sections and categories, they will be automatically placed on these pages according to the parameters you set for each page.

55

For example, you have a Section Blog layout for "Food" section, and let's assume you have it set to order articles starting with the most recent one first. When you add a new Article to the "Food" Section, it will automatically show on the "Food" blog page as the first Article. You don't have to do anything other than add the Article and assign it to the "Food "Section. Remember you already have created your sections before.

Organizing Articles in Article Manager

If you will have a large number of articles on your site, a second reason to use sections and categories is to simply group the articles so you can find them. For example, in the Article Manager, you can filter articles based on Section or Category. Therefore, if you have 300 articles in your site, you can find an Article more easily if you know its Section or Category it belongs to.

Creating a Section and Category

To practically create a section in your Joomla! Back-end, do the following steps which I have identified earlier in this chapter. I placed them here again for your convenience. Login to you Joomla! Administrator Panel and click on "Section Manager" or on the Content⟶Section Manager.

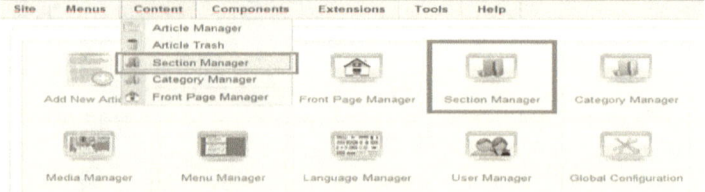

1. Click on New on the top right of the "Section Manager".

2. Enter the following fields:

Chapter Three - Understanding Sections and Categories

- **Title:** The name of the section. This will show as page headings if you have the settings to show this.

- **Alias:** A unique name for the section, not shown on any pages (Optional).

- **Published:** Select **Yes** to enable the section for use on the website or **No** to disable the use.

- **Access Level:** Determines who in your site can use this section. Public is everybody, Registered is anyone who has an account with your site and Special are editors, publishers, managers and above.

- **Image:** A selection of images for the section, if used, it will show on pages (Optional).

- **Image Position:** Relative to the Title

- **Description:** Describes what the section is and what it is used for. While it is optional, it is recommended, especially when you have a number of administrators looking after your website. They will know what the section is all for (Optional).

3. After filling up the fields. Click **Save**. You will see the title of the section you just created in the "Section Manager" list.

57

Now you can create a Category and Place them under Section we have created earlier. To do this, simply:

1. Navigate to Content⟶Category Manager.

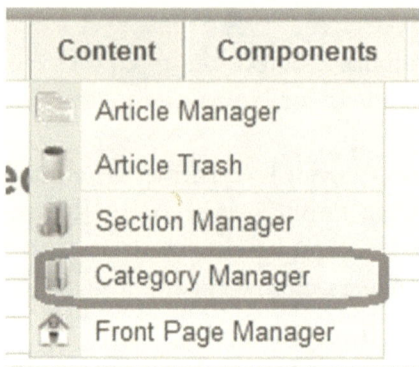

2. Click the New button in the Category Manager:[content].

3. Fill out the fields in the same manner as we did in "Creating the Section".

    Title: The name of the Category. This is what will show on the pages if needed

    Alias: A unique name for the Category. It is not shown anywhere. If left blank, Joomla! will fill it in automatically (Optional).

    Published: Select **Yes** to enable the category, **No** to disable it,

    Section: This is where you select the section you want. Select the Section title that you created earlier. This depends on how many sections you have created and to which section you want to contain the category.

    Category order: While there are no fields showing at the moment, when you place your second category in under the section, you can select the order of the categories here.

Access Level: Set to who you want to see the category, Public is everybody, Registered is everybody who has registered to your site and Special are managers access and up.

Image: Displays and Image next to the Category Title on the web pages with the Category Title Showing (Optional),

Image Location: Where the image is located relative to the title.

Description: Describe what the Category is and what it is used for. While this is optional, it is recommended in case other site administrators try to use the Category (Optional).

4. When all fields have been completed, click the **Save** button.

5. After all the steps, When you go to the *Article Manager* and select the *Section* that you created, the category list will show the Categories assigned to that Section

To add more categories, repeat the steps described above. Same applies to section if you wish to add more sections to your Joomla! site.

Joomla! is an advanced content management system, but unless you understand how to properly organize and manage your content, you make many of Joomla!'s advanced features useless. Take the time to develop your content structure first, and you will save yourself a lot of time and effort later.

Chapter Four

Making your site Dynamic with Component, Modules & Plugins

In this chapter, we shall be discussing the components and extensions. However, Joomla! comes with pre-installed components and extensions like the Banner, Contact, Search components etc. It also comes with some Module like the Login Module, Bread Crumbs, Footer and so on.

What is a Component in Joomla!?

Component is one of the extension in Joomla!. Components are the main functional units of Joomla! and they can be seen as mini-applications. The components are Joomla!'s content elements or applications that are usually displayed in the center of the main content area of a template. However, this depends on the design of the template you are using. Components are core elements of Joomla!'s functionality. These core elements include Banners, Contact, Polls, and Banner Component.

Components and Extension

To really make your site look good and function well, you will have to use the Joomla! Extended functionalities which mean that you will be using Components and Extensions menu in the back-end of your Joomla! site. However, the key difference between the two is that components are more powerful and more complex; they are actually applications within the Joomla! applications. Modules are smaller add-ons that can contain all sorts of dynamic information and sometimes components and Modules are designed to work together. However, the secret is that both component and extensions generally serve the same purpose in the back-end of your Joomla! site. They enhance your website functionalities.

Chapter Four - Making your site Dynamic with Component, Modules & Plugins

The components and extension we shall be using here are the ones that Joomla! has already. Joomla! comes with some basic components and extension that you can make use of.

You might want to add some extensions to make your site even more functional and attractive. There are thousands of useful ones on the web, providing you with whatever requirement you might need in your website. Some are free and some are commercial; visit http://extensions. joomla.org for more.

Adding the Contact Component

When you have a website and you do not properly show where you can be contacted, you are creating doubt in the minds of your users. This is a very important component in every website as it enables visitors to get in touch through a contact form. To add this, you have two major steps to follow.

- **First**: You will create a contact.

- **Second**: You will create a menu link that will display the contact form in the front-end of your site. Let's work it out and add a contact to the site:

    1. Navigate to Components—>Contacts. You will be shown the contact manager. Click **New**

    2. Enter the details in the Contact: [New] screen. Put the name of the contact.

    3. In the category drop down list, select 'Contact'.

4. Enter all contact information you wish to appear. This depends on your wish, but better fill out the email and telephone box. Make sure you specify a valid email address, because it is where the form data or rather the message will be sent to.

5. Other information are not mandatory, however, you can add some little details on the miscellaneous information box. It serves as an introductory text on the form page.

6. All other parameters depend on your requirement.

7. Now click **Save**.

💡 To be able to create a contact form to your site, you have to first create a contact. Using the contact component, you can build a very comprehensive system of contact organized by contact categories. However, just one contact name and email address will be enough.

Creating the Contact form Menu link

1. Simply navigate to Menus⟶ Main menu and click on the **New** button.

2. Select "Contacts-Standard" contact layout in the Menu item type.

3. Write the title for the menu item, for example (CONTACT) this will show on the main menu items in the front-end of the site.

4. Select in the drop down the contact you just created in the Parameter Basics. (Simon J). see image below:

Chapter Four - Making your site Dynamic with Component, Modules & Plugins

5. In the **Parameter (system)** section, just add a page title. Example like **(Contact us)** this will be displayed at the top of the contact form.

6. Click the **Save** button and you are now having a Contact link in your website.

7. Preview the changes in your site.

You have just used the contact components in Joomla! to create a contact and actually added a menu link to a contact form. When a visitor clicks on it in the site, it displays a contact form where they can keep in touch with you. This has, again, proved how powerful menu links are in Joomla!. Just by selecting menu item types: **Standard Contact Layout,** you have successfully created a menu link that takes a visitor to a contact form page. It's so easy and interesting; the power of Joomla!

Adding the Poll Component

When you create a website, polls are good way of adding a quick iterative element to your website. Joomla! has this functionality built in which allows a simple survey of multiple choice questions for visitors.

65

This could be on product or services your provide. To add polls simply follow these steps:

1. Go to Component-Polls. In the "Poll Manager" screen and click New button at the top right of the page.

2. Click on the Published button to YES to enable the display of the poll in the site front-end

3. Unchanged the Lag. This allows visitor to vote once in a day.

4. Enter the details of the survey. However, in the title box, enter the Question you want visitor to vote on as the title example: (Joomla! is used for?)

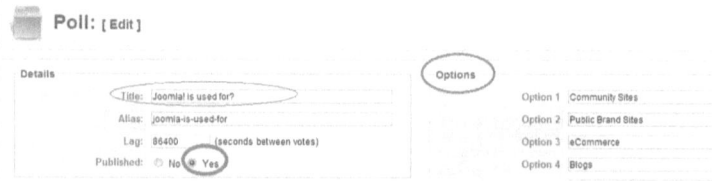

5. Add the possible answers in the **Option** Section and click **Save**.

You have just created the Poll in the back-end of Joomla! Now, you need to do one more process which is to display the poll in the front-end of the site. The Poll component and Poll Module are related and here depend on each other to function well. The Module tells Joomla! on what pages the poll should appear and what position it should be displayed within the site. To do this:

1. Go to Extension⟶Module Manager and click on New.

2. Click the Poll Module in the Module [New] screen. You may either click on the poll name or radio button and click Next.

3. Type Polls in the title or any one that suits you. (However, for this one, we are using Polls).

Chapter Four - Making your site Dynamic with Component, Modules & Plugins

4. Click show Title: Yes.

5. Click on enable to: Yes.

6. Select the Position you want the module to be displayed on your site.

7. To show the Poll only in the Home page, click on select menu item(s) form the List. And Select "Home" under main menu. However, if you wish to display the poll in every page of the website simply click on menus: "All".

8. Select the Poll you have created in the module parameters and click **Save**.

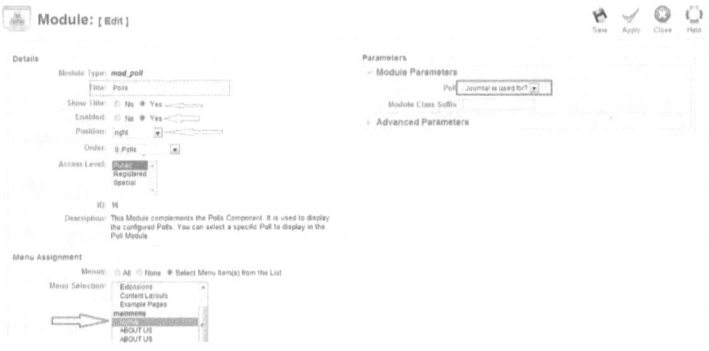

9. Click Preview to see changes in your site front-end. Note that we only select home to show the polls. The Polls will not be shown in any other page within the site.

You now have a poll on your site which will allow visitors to select one option and vote by clicking the **Vote** button, and can view the result in the main content screen.

Creating the Search Component

Even the best design navigation will confuse some people; you have to give your visitors a way of searching your site by "key word". In this section we will create a menu and linking it to the search component. To do this simply:

1. Go to Menus→Main Menu and click New.

2. In the Menu item type, click Search. The only layout option available is the search component itself, so click Search again.

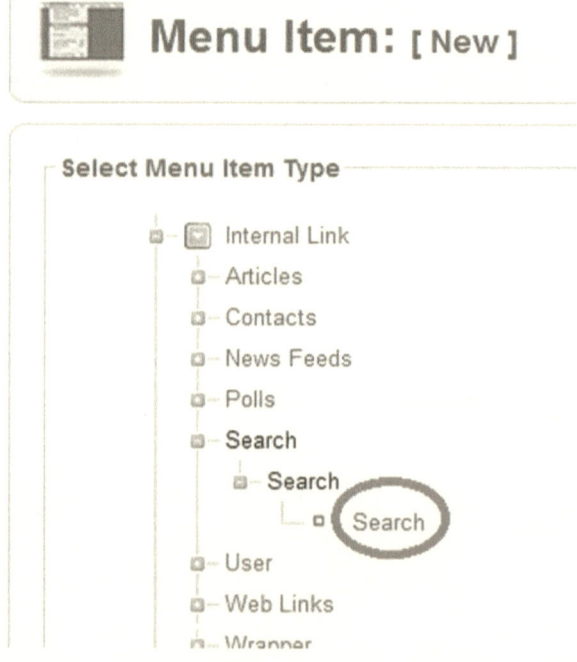

3. You will be shown the Menu item [New]. Enter the title, in this case type "search this site".

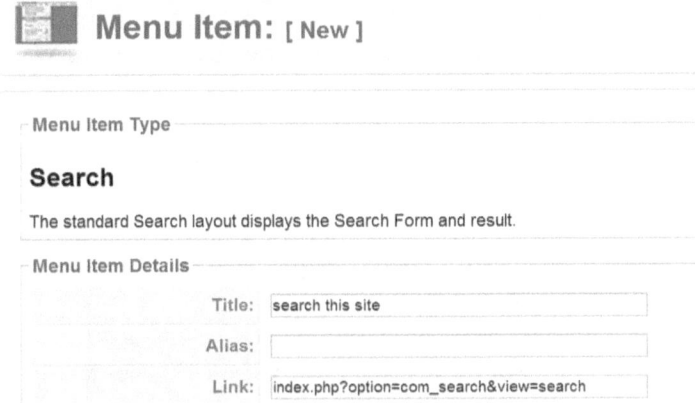

4. Click **Save**.

5. Click Preview to see the changes on your site and click on the "search this site" link in the menu.

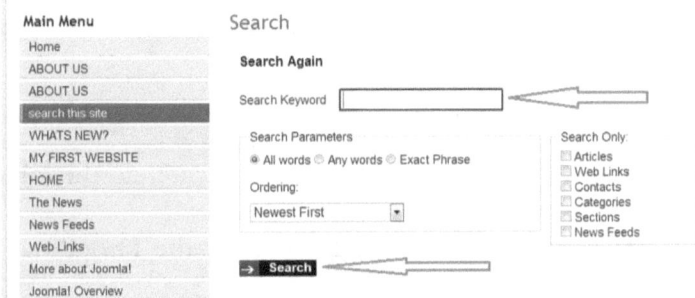

Joomla! search component searches data's stored across the site. You can link directly to the component or add a search module which visitors can use to start searches.

The Banner Component

In most websites, Banners are a very popular way of advertising, especially for website that makes sales online. Joomla! has banner placement and organizational capabilities as a basic feature. This component is designed so that the webmaster can easily manipulate with banner exchange. The webmaster has information on the number of clicks, i.e, will have a stored count of how many people click on the banner and can also set certain banner categories as well as give authority to the clients he/she chooses.

To begin this process, you have to make configuration for the banner component in the back-end of your Joomla! when you click on the banner, you will notice three submenu that will be visible i.e. Banner, Clients, Categories. See the following Picture:

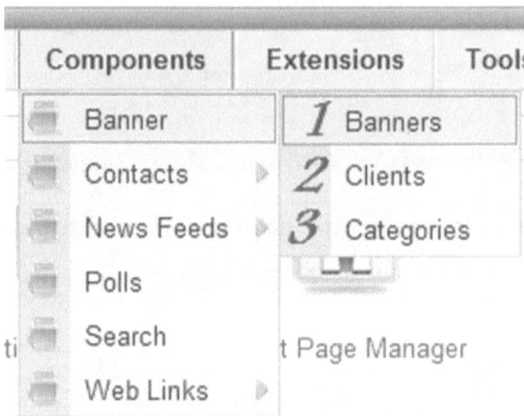

- To create a *Banner* on your Joomla! website, do the following:

    1. Select Component⟶Banner on the Dropdown menu of the components.

    2. Select Categories⟶Click on **Add New** on the top right of the page.

    3. Fill up all necessary details and click **Save**.

Chapter Four - Making your site Dynamic with Component, Modules & Plugins

↘ To create a banner, you must create a category after which you add the client's details and finally setting the Banner.

- The next step is the *Clients*, here you enter the details of the clients which are the client title, the name of its company or organization and contact e-mail. You may also consider entering Extra information on the right hand side. See image below:

- The main purpose is to create a banner for the website; however, banner is the main option for creating your Banners. In this section, the Basic Details/parameters for the banner presentation are name, category, client name, custom banner code, impressions and click URL. After doing that, click **Save** on the top right of the page.

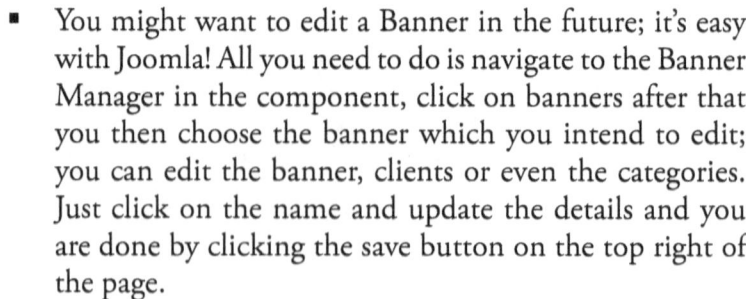

You'll notice that there is an image preview at the bottom; it is one of the default banners from the 1.5 version (this book is all about 1.5 Joomla! version). Those pictures are loaded from Joomla!'s media/banners root directory. If you want to use your own banners, you can put your pictures into this directory and they will appear in the appropriate drop-down menu, available for selection. But make sure when you upload your own picture i.e. the banner, it should be on the banner Folder under the Media manager in the Joomla! back-end.

- You might want to edit a Banner in the future; it's easy with Joomla! All you need to do is navigate to the Banner Manager in the component, click on banners after that you then choose the banner which you intend to edit; you can edit the banner, clients or even the categories. Just click on the name and update the details and you are done by clicking the save button on the top right of the page.

- To create Banners, you must click on the New button on the top right of every submenu page on the banner component.

- The custom banner code is a code that you put there to represent the banner that will be displayed on the website. Some banners can be in codes; however this option will convert the code to physical image on the website.

Caution: Make sure you set the "Show Banner" parameter to **Yes** or else your banner will not be displayed.

- After setting the parameters, go to the Module Manager and select the Banners Module (mod_banners) which must be used in conjunction with the Banners Component.

The Banners Module is responsible for displaying results on the front-end which is the main site. First, we have to adjust the module itself. There are options for defining the position of the banners, their order, the access level, the category, the client and various other options as displayed on the next image.

Generally, Modules help you make and administer your site. Joomla! has many different Modules in it and modules can display information on pages of your site.

➤ The Modules can only be used inside your administrator panel. This means that you cannot modify any part of the module from the front-end.

The Banner Module

This Module usually comes with the Joomla! 1.5version installed in it. However, the module shows the Banners on your site when you set a position of the module. Let's assume the banner module is set to show on syndicate position of the template, and then the banners (image) will show on syndicate also in the front end. Look at the next image.

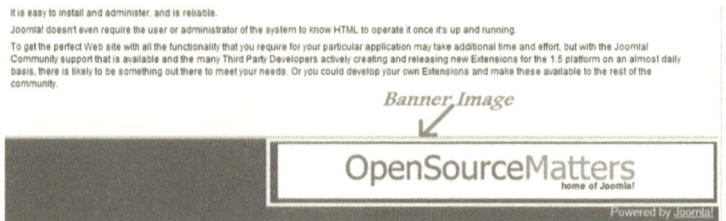

This Banner is set to be in the syndicate position of the module. You may set your banners in any position available in the template. However, you don't have to limit your banner position to the "Banner Position" of your template. Set it to any position you wish providing it will enhance the looks of your website. You can set how many times you intend to show the banner.

➤ Templates are different in design and positions. Some do have many module positions and some have just few. So you will have to check the positions available in the template before you assign a Module position.

Setting the Module (Banner)

For a better result and display of the banner in the front-end, you will have to set the Modules; this Module has three parts.

Chapter Four - Making your site Dynamic with Component, Modules & Plugins

1. Details
2. Menu Assignment
3. Module Parameters

1. Details

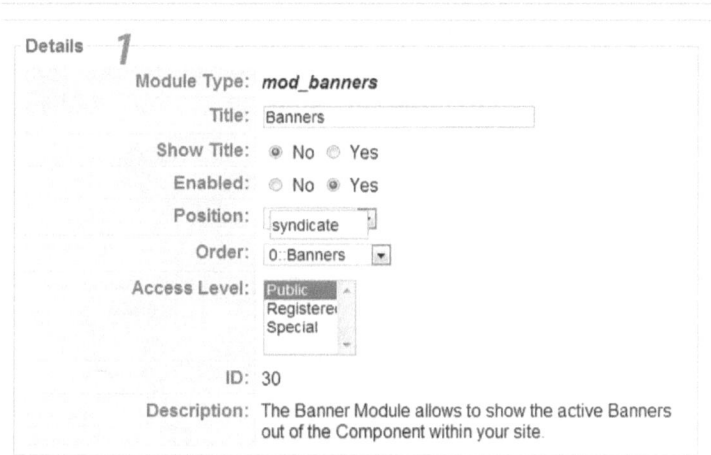

- ✓ **Module Type**: Displays the name of module file.

- ✓ **Title**: The Module Name to be displayed in the site.

- ✓ **Show title**: Shows the name of Module.

- ✓ **Enabled**: Enables the use of this modulewill be visible in the front-end.

- ✓ **Position**: Changes the position of the module on the site.

- ✓ **Order**: Modifies module alignment options.

- ✓ **Access Level**: Changes the category of members who have permission to use the module. Select any one of the list.

- ✓ **ID**: Displays the ID of Module.

- ✓ **Description**: Shows a short description of the module.

2. Menu Assignment

This gives you the flexibility to have more than one banner on a page. The Banner Module can be assigned to any other module position not just the banner's position, although some cannot be used more than once on a page.

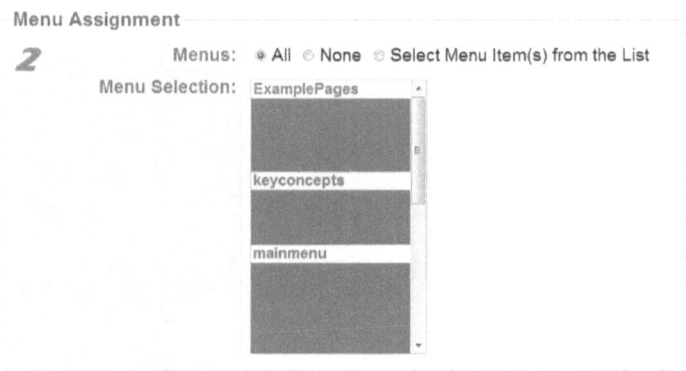

- ✓ **Menus**: Options available.

- ✓ **All**: Show the banners in all menus and pages.

- ✓ **None**: Do not show the banners on site.

- ✓ **Select Menu Item(s) from the list**: Gives you the privilege to Select menu and menu objects that you want to show your banners.

3. Parameters

This part is also an important part of the Banner Module Setting. This Module has options to open a link on banners in a new tab, a new window, or same window. You will see this action in the next screenshot.

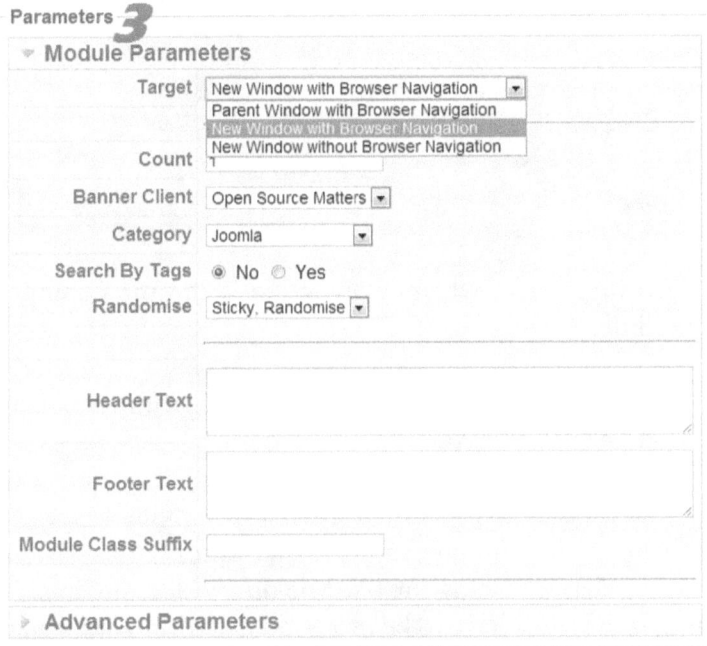

- ✓ **Target**: The target window when it is clicked.

- ✓ **Count**: The number of banners to display.

- ✓ **Banner Client**: Show banners only from a selected client.

- ✓ **Category**: Show banners only from a selected category.

- ✓ **Search by tags**: The banner is selected by matching the banner's tags to the current document keywords.

- ✓ **Randomize**: Randomize the ordering of the banner.

- ✓ **Header Text**: A heading to display before the group of banners.

- ✓ **Footer text**: The text to display after the group of banners.

- ✓ **Module Class Suffix**: A suffix to be applied to the CSS class of the module, which allows individual module styling.

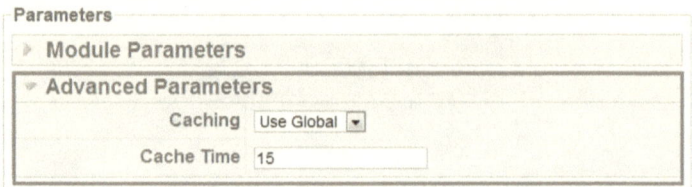

- ✓ **Caching**: Select whether or not to cache the content of this module.

- ✓ **Caching Time**: The period of time, in minutes, before the module is re-cached.

Having done the whole process, you need to provide a proper "sight" of the other part of your site to your site visitors. The best and easy way for doing that is placing the banners on a visible site location. The main thing is that they have to be in a good place but with fewer colors; simple but nice; focus on fonts. There are a few options when it comes to banner type; you can choose if it's going to be static or dynamic. Static means only text with no effects. Recently, the most popular ones are GIF and Flash banners. GIFs are better for SEO in distinction from Flash formats.

Understanding Modules

When you install Joomla! about 20 built-in Modules are available for use in the front-end of your web site. Some Modules, like the Menu Module, are used in every Joomla! web site. Other Modules are optional. This is where you will add new Modules or edit existing Modules for the front-end of your Joomla! website. In this section, you will learn how to create a Sidebar and Login Modules. You will also learn how to configure the Modules.

Modules are the blocks of content in your site and are distinctively separate from your main content area. For example, a Module may appear to the left, right, top, or down or below your main article content. The Module Manager allows you to customize each Module to your **"Preference"**. Each Module in Joomla! has some constant features. Below are the fields you will see in every Joomla! Module. Modules have more individual parameters but these are the most important ones to understand first.

- Title
- Show Title
- Enabled
- Position
- Module Class Suffix
- Menu Assignment
- Ordering

Title:

The title of the module is displayed above the module on the frontend. It's also called a "Module Heading". After a Module is saved, the module's title is also shown in the Joomla! back-end administration.

Show Title:

This setting allows you to specify whether or not the module's title should be visible on the frontend.

Enabled:

Allows you to enable (or publish) the selected module. To enable a module only on specific pages, see below Menu Assignment.

Position:

A Module position may be labeled as left, right, bottom, top, etc.

Module positions are defined by the template. If a Module is published in a position that is not supported by the template, it will not show up. It is important to be aware of your template's supported module positions. In Joomla! 1.5, only the module positions of the default template are available in the module manager.

Module Class Suffix:

A Module class suffix allows you to specify a preset style which is defined by the template. You'll need to consult your individual template documentation to see what module styles/suffixes are available. This is beyond the scope of this book.

(See also: How to apply a Module Class Suffix)

Menu Assignment:

When a Module is enabled it can be assigned to all pages or pages specified in the Menu Assignment dialog.

 Modules can only assigned to pages that have menu items.

Ordering:

You can set the order of a Module to appear in the ordering dialog as well as the Module Manager main page by clicking the up/down arrows.

Chapter Four - Making your site Dynamic with Component, Modules & Plugins

All Modules have two sections that are the same: Details and Menu Assignment. The Parameters are different for each Module type.

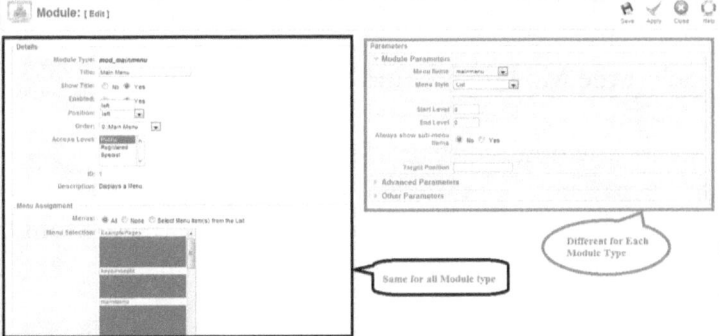

Creating a Sidebar

In this section, you will learn how to create a Module to display your content to your website as a sidebar. You might want to add your "working hours" displayed on your site. This is how you do it:

1. Go to Extension→Module Manager and click New. You will see about 20 or so Modules available.

2. Choose or click the Custom HTML Module.

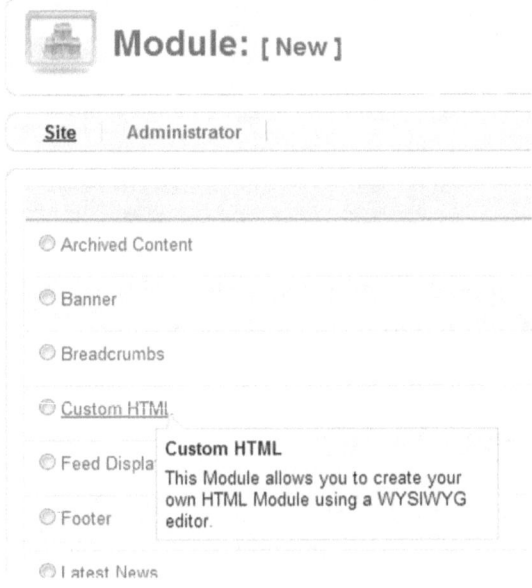

81

3. Enter the title of the Module.

4. Click on Enabled to Yes.

5. Select the Module Position.

6. Leave any other settings as it is.

7. Scroll down to the bottom of the page. In the Custom Output Area, type the Working Hours. See next image:

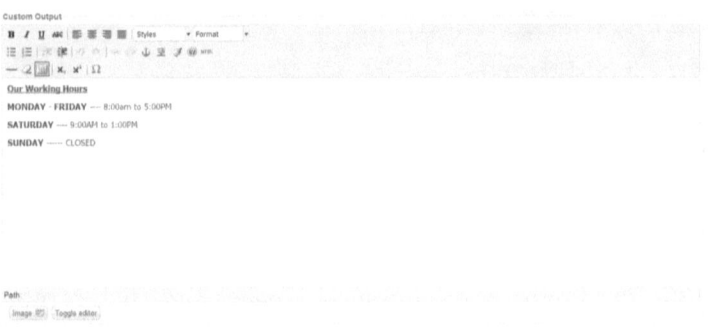

8. Click **Save**.

9. Click on Preview at the top right of the page to see the changes on your site.

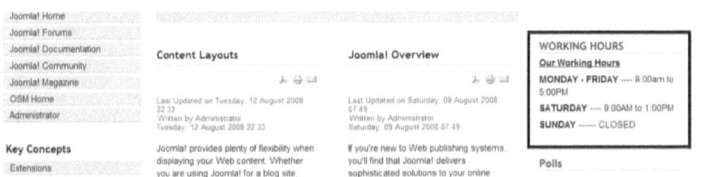

You have now successfully added a sidebar using the custom Module to display your Working Hours on your website.

Creating a Login Module

Login, Polls, Breadcrumbs, site searches are just some of the few pre-programmed Module types that comes with Joomla! 1.5. However, you

Chapter Four - Making your site Dynamic with Component, MODULES & Plugins

will learn how to create a Login Module to your site which allows your visitors to register an account with you and login to the website. To do this:

1. Go to Extension—➤Module Manager and click New. You will see about 20 or so Modules available.

2. Select the login Module. You can either click on it or select the radio button and click Next.

3. Enter the title of the Module.

4. Click on Enabled to Yes.

5. Select the Module Position.

You may want to add some details in the Parameters. Remember the parameters of every Module are different as we have seen earlier.

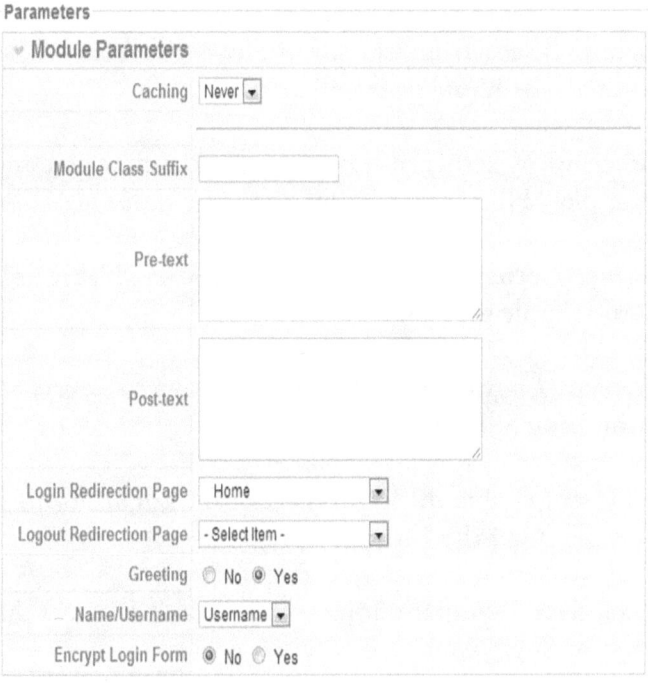

83

- **Caching.** Caching is not allowed, so "Never" is always selected.

- **Module Class Suffix.** A suffix applied to the CSS class of the Module. This allows you to create customized CSS styles that will apply just to this module. You would then modify the "template.css" file of your template to apply styling to this new class

- **Pre-text.** Optional text or HTML to display above the login form.

- **Post-text.** Optional text or HTML to display below the login form.

- **Login Redirection Page.** The page to load after a successful login. Select from the drop-down list box. If no page is selected, the home page will be used.

- **Logout Redirection Page.** The page to load after a successful logout. Select from the drop-down list box. If no page is selected, the home page will be used.

- **Greeting.** Whether or not to show the simple greeting text, for example, "Hi Administrator".

- **Name/Username.** Whether to use the user's Name or Username in the simple greeting.

- **Encrypt Login Form.** Whether or not to encrypt the login form using SSL.

Caution: Do not enable this option (Encrypt Login Form) if Joomla! is not accessible using the "https://" prefix.

6. Click **Save** if you are done setting it and Preview the changes on your Site.

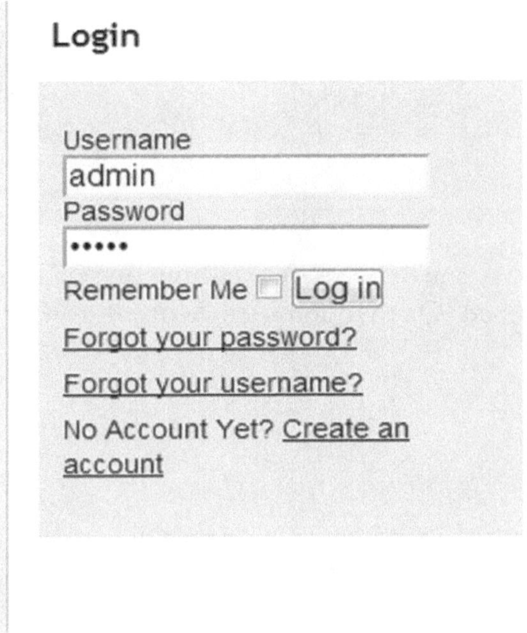

Chapter Four - Making your site Dynamic with Component, Modules & Plugins

Login

Username: admin
Password: •••••
Remember Me ☐ Log in
Forgot your password?
Forgot your username?
No Account Yet? Create an account

You have successfully created a login form to your website and visitors can create an account with you. The registered members can login any time they visit your website.

Practically all Modules are configured the same way, but remember! The parameters for each Module are different. So you have to set the parameters for each Module you want to add on your website.

Other Modules you will see in Joomla! are as follows; you might want to add any of them to your website to make it more meaningful and functional for your visitors.

Breadcrumbs

This Module shows a set of navigation links that illustrate where you are inside the website and allows you to navigate back. An example is shown in the next image.

You are here: Home ▶ MY FIRST WEBSITE ▶ MORE ABOUT JOOMLA

NewsFlash

This Module shows one or more Articles from one Category each time the page is refreshed. One random Article or a list of Articles can be displayed.

Random Image

This Module displays a random image from a directory. Could be from any folder you created in the **Media Manger.**

Related Articles

This Module shows a list of Articles that are related to the current Article being viewed by the user (for example, an Article Layout or a Blog or List layout where the user has clicked on an Article link). Articles are considered to be related to each other if they share at least one Keyword in the Article's Metadata Information.

Syndicate

This Module creates a RSS Feed link for the page. This allows a User to create a newsfeed for the current page. An example is shown below.

Who's Online

This Module displays information about Users currently browsing the website. See example below.

> **Who's Online**
> We have 1 guest online

Wrapper

This Module allows you to insert an external web site into an IFrame at the Module position. If the web page is bigger than the Module size, scroll bars can be displayed.

Footer

This Module displays the web site copyright information, see example below.

> Copyright © 2011 My First Website. All Rights Reserved.
> Joomla! is Free Software released under the GNU/GPL License.

Latest News

This Module shows a list of the most recently published Articles in your site.

> **Latest News**
> Joomla! License Guidelines
> Content Layouts
> The Joomla! Community
> Welcome to Joomla!
> Newsflash 4

Some Joomla! Extensions provide new Module Types. If you have installed any Extensions, your Joomla! site might have Module Types that are not listed here. In this case, please refer to the documentation of the Extension for information about these Module Types, i.e., the one you installed. We shall talk about Extension in the last chapter of this book.

Understanding the Plug-in

Plugins are used to handle login, text replacement, editors and other functions. Plugins are an essential but rarely noticed part of Joomla! Plugins are very flexible and can execute for various purposes at many different times. To locate the plugin Manager, Go to Extensions—➤Plugin Manager, you will see the list of the plugins available on the system. The plugin covers a wide variety of functionalities, you will notice on the top of the list the Authentication Plugins, for example if you want to enable your visitors to login to your sire Using their GMAIL Username and Password. Simply enable the AuthenticationGmail by clicking on the **Red Cross** to make it a **Green tick**.

Some of the editor-Plugin helps to display the button that we use in the content of our site. When you install Joomla! 1.5, there is pre-installed plugin and Joomla! has set them the best way for you. However, you might want to edit some of the plugins, so simply click on the plugin and edit it and then click Save. If you want to make the plugin function in your site, make sure you set it as "enabled" or else you won't be able to see any changes in your site. Remember not all plugins have a physical effect on your website, but they are very important for your site. To read more about plugins, go to:

- ✓ http://forum.joomla.org Sign up for the forums, search, and ask questions, even helping others if you are able!

- ✓ http://help.joomla.org Find more documentation and training information.

Caution:

- If you don't know about a particular plugin, DO NOT make any changes to it.

- Do not delete any plugin that comes with Joomla! during installation.

When you install some extensions, they might not function on your site. However, you will have to enable the System Legacy in the Plugin Manager (usually on the number 25 of the plugin List). Some extensions are for older version of Joomla! but are compatible to Joomla 1.5 only if you enable the system legacy.

Chapter Five

Managing Front-end & Back-end Users

In every site, if there are no users then it's considered useless. You need someone who will manage the website and also other users which could be a customer or a guest. Managing the registered users of your website can be a time-consuming process, especially if you have a large number of users, all of whom have different roles to perform. Each role or user profile has access to certain information or tasks (if they're administrative) within the scope of your website. You have the tools to determine the extent of their access by using the back-end interface Modules. To give you clearer picture of what we are saying, we'll use the "My First Website" website to show you how to manage your users and their profiles.

In this chapter, we will look at the User Manager to deal with different situations that will arise in your role as content editor and web master. These include:

- ❖ Managing the existing front-end and administrative users
- ❖ Creating and editing new user accounts
- ❖ Managing username and password problems
- ❖ Dealing with annoying users
- ❖ Communicating with various users
- ❖ And more.

You might be wondering who these Users are. Users are set of people who have registered their information/ details with you in your website and are allocated access to certain information, depending on their role within the scope of your website. They can be administrators and content editors/contributors (from the back-end perspective) or customers (front-end) who buy your product and services.

There are visitor who just visit your website often and you feel you have something to offer them. For example, you want to provide special promotion to only those who are genuinely interested in your services or products. Encouraging them to register allows you to collect contact information and keep in touch. Probably you can convert it into a contentious relationship with sales and benefits for your business.

Furthermore, users are your website visitors, content contributors, and administrators. Contributors here mean those that can add article to the website from the front-end, and the administrators will have most of their functions in the back-end of the website, but they also can contribute from the front-end. This depends on the access level given to each User.

The Back-end Users (Administrators)

These users can edit and update the content of your site by logging into the administration control panel of the website. The Administrator Manager or Super Administrator access both is different with specific access. For example, the Super Administrators have absolute control over the website while the Administrative manager does not have absolute access to the website; he has limited access. For example, he cannot access the global configuration of the website in the back-end. However, there are various levels of access within the administration control panel, the highest level being the Super Administrator.

The Website Users (Front-end Users)

These users do not have access to the administration panel, i.e., the back-end unlike the Super Administrator and can only access material and information through the actual front-end. These users can be:

1. Guests or casual visitors to your site. These visitors come to your site anonymously and unregistered.

2. Registered users, authors, editors, and publishers who are been given the privileges to edit and update information only from the frontend.

3. People who register their details in order to subscribe, buy or transact with you.

When a user is registered with you, they are allocated to a group; this is based on the settings applied within the Global Configuration. This gives permission to visitors to register on your website to become registered member of the site. They can be any one of the following:

- ✓ **Registered Users**: These are visitors to your site who have registered themselves in order to view certain content or transact with you.

- ✓ **Authors**: These are users that can submit new content articles to the site with approval, but can't edit existing articles. An administrator or person that holds a higher access level must approve before submissions.

- ✓ **Editors**: These users can submit and edit new content articles. A publisher or someone higher must also approve these entries.

- ✓ **Publishers**: These types of users can submit new content articles, edit existing articles, and publish the articles without any permission or approval.

None of the above mentioned user groups have access to the administration back-end of the website, and can only edit or add material from the front-end.

Disallowing User to Register Accounts on your site

By default, Joomla! sets the user setting to allow users to create account, but then you as the sole owner of the website and the super Administrator of the site, might want to stop users from creating account from the front-end. If you don't want to allow users to create an account on your site, this is how you set it:

1. Navigate to the *Global Configuration panel* in the top menu.

2. Select the *<System—>* tab only. See screenshot below.

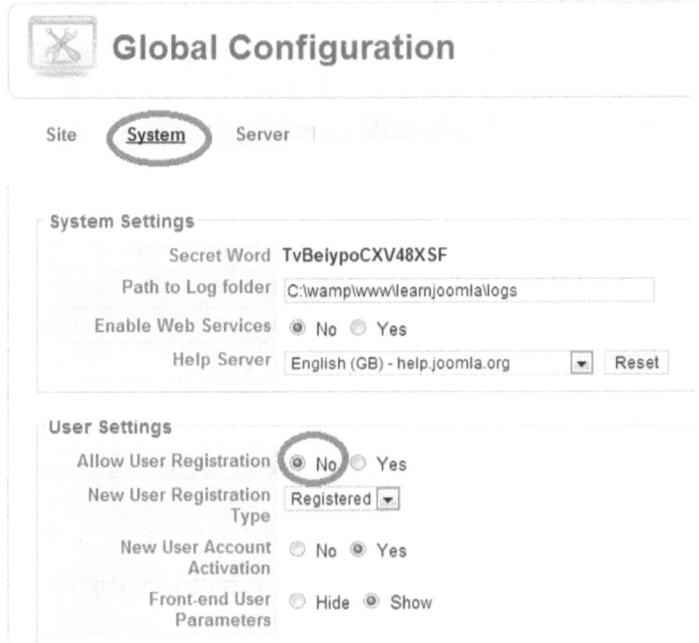

3. Click **Save** button on the top right of the page.

4. To view the changes on your site front-end, click on the Preview link on the top right of the page, when this is done, a new tab should open on your browser and you will be able to view the changes. The next image shows the final result.

You will observe that the "create account" link is missing; you only have the "forgot your password" and "forgot your username" links. This is because you have set the 'allow user registration' to be **No** in the Global configuration of the user setting.

Editing the Login Form in the front-end

From the front-end of your website, the Login Form allows users to access content that is potentially spared for them and can only be visible to them; this can also be to make payment or purchase items from your site if you're running an e-commerce site. You can also customize your Login Form by adding text and a link to create new accounts for potential Users who wish to register.

Forgotten usernames and passwords

These links are very important not only for users to find their password or username again, but also to help you to manage users. Rather than unnecessarily creating a new account if they have lost their login details, to reset there details and send to their email for future login is the best way to handle this.

When a user clicks any of the above links it will generate a request to enter an e-mail address. This confirms the e-mail and verification token will be sent to that e-mails which allows the user to enter and reset their password.

Allowing User to Register Accounts on your site

To allow user registration in your website, you have to apply the following steps:

1. Navigate to the Global Configuration panel in the top menu.

2. Select the⟶System tab. only.

3. Go to the User Setting

4. Click **Yes** for 'Allow User Registration'. This will add the "Create an account" link to the frontend Login Form.

➤ You can change it to 'No' anytime you want, but mind you, only existing member will be able to login. No one can register.

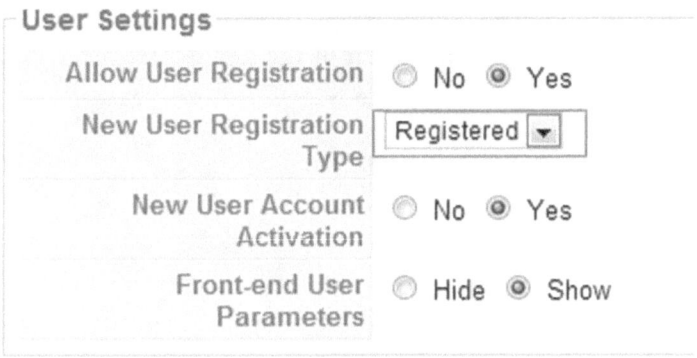

5. Open 'New User Registration' Type. Here you allocate these new users as Registered for New User Registration Type.

6. Click **Yes** for New User Account Activation to send an e-mail to the new user requesting them to activate their registration before gaining access. You might set it to NO if you want to ease the stress of your new user.

💡 This helps protect against malicious and unnecessary registrations.

7. Click **Hide** or **Show** for the Front-end User Parameters, which provide options for the new user to set their preferred settings when they log in.

8. Click **Save**.

Adding custom text to the Login Form

You can add customized text to the top and bottom part of the Login Form using the Modules menu. To do this:

1. Navigate to Extensions⟶Module Manager through the top menu.

2. Click on the Login under the Module Name column to open its screen. If you have named it something else other than login, then select that name. The Details and Menu Assignment sections contain the settings, positioning, and details of the actual login form is shown in the next screenshot.

Chapter Five - Managing Front-end & Back-end Users

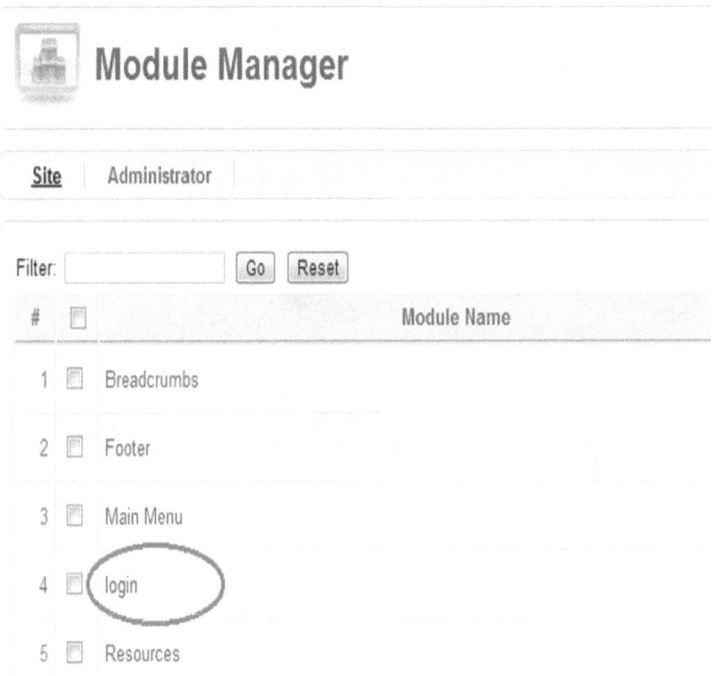

3. When you click on it, you will see the next page. You can change any of the setting you wish, or else, just leave it the way they are.

99

4. Go to the **Parameters** section to the right of screen, as shown in the following screenshot, and add your text in the Pre-text and Post-text input boxes. The Pre-text is the text that is displayed before the Username and Post-text is displayed at the end.

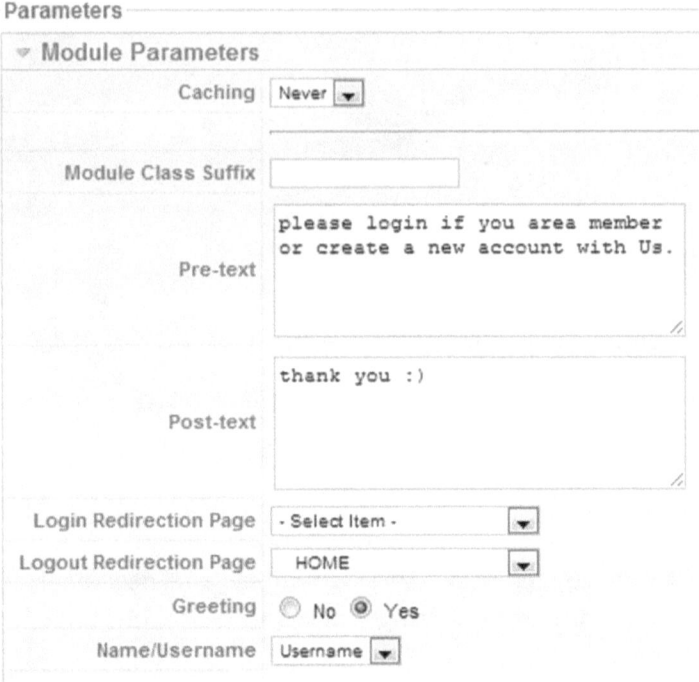

5. Click **Save** at the top right of the page. You should now see the changes as shown in the following screenshot.

Redirecting registered users to a certain pages of the site

In the Module parameter within the login Module, you can also set which page will be displayed when a user logs in and what page displays after logging out. This can be a very useful tool and you can create a discount page for your customer or important information page for them to see when they login or log out. To perform these settings, do the following:

1. Click Login Redirection Page in the Parameters section and select any page you wish a user to be shown when he/she login.

2. Click Logout Redirection Page in the Parameters section and Select any page you wish a user to be shown when he/she logs out.

3. Decide whether to show or hide a short greeting.

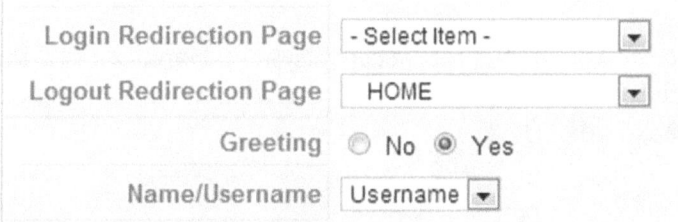

4. Click **Apply** to implement the changes. Navigate to the "Preview" link at the top-right of the page to view your site in the browser.

5. Click **Save** if you are satisfied with the changes.

Creating a new User to your Site

Assuming you are the super administrator of the website and you wish to have an assistant, but not having the same access as you have. You as the super Administrator want to add a user with the Manager Access level; you can do this by doing the following:

1. Click Site⟶Control panel⟶Click the User Manager on the front page of the administration page.

2. To add a new user, *click* the new icon on the top right page.

3. Type in the name, a username, an e-mail address, and a password into the Name, Username, and New Password input boxes, as shown in the following screenshot. Verify the password to be sure you have entered the correct string.

4. Click on the user group that you want to allocate them to from the selection in the Group window. Your choice will obviously depend upon the content and access level you want them to have. We shall select Manager in this case.

5. Click **No** for Block User, as we are setting up a new one.

6. Select **Yes** or **No** for Receive System E-mails. As a manager, selecting Yes will allow him receive internal E-mails from the back-end.

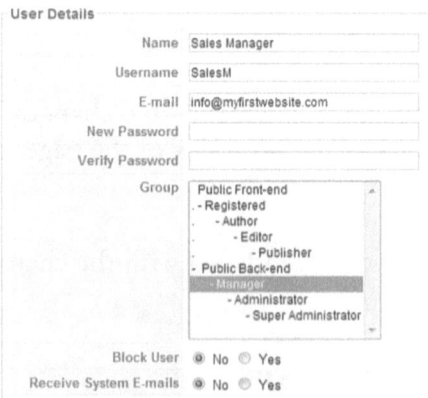

7. Click **Save** at the top right of the page and your new user is created.

Adding a new Customer Manually

When you want to add a customer to site as a registered member, just follow the same steps as described in the "Creating a new user to your Site" above.

➤ You will have to select the Group to "**Registered**" in this case because the user is a customer and can only access the site from the front-end. He has no access whatsoever to the back-end of the website.

Editing existing users

This process is very easy to do; just do the following steps:

- Click the name of the user in the list on the User Manager screen.

- Make all necessary changes you want to do and click **Save**.

➤ If you have many users and user groups on your site. You can use the filtering option to select the group you want to edit.

Resetting a username and password

Registered front-end users can do this for themselves using one of the links in the Login Form. Alternatively, you can use the 'User Manager' again to edit the users profile details. You can do this especially for the back-end users, example: Manager or administrator, following these steps:

- Navigate to the User Manager screen.

- Select User and open the profile screen.

- Enter the new password in the Password input box then verify it.

- **Save** the changes when you're done.

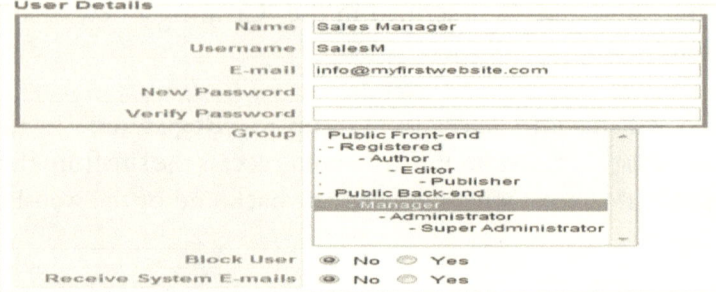

Dealing with annoying users

Sometimes you need to block a user's access to the site because of their act. Some users are spam and register themselves to the site. In this case, you have to delete them. However, if you have a particular individual user (registered user—not a spam but is annoying) to take action on, the best method for handling this is to disable the account rather than deleting it.

To Delete a User

- Navigate to the 'User Manager' screen; click the User Manager icon on the administration control panel.

- Click on the user you wish to delete in the list of the user. If the users are too many, use the filter to get the user group.

- Click the Delete icon at the top right menu to remove that user profile.

In the same page, you will notice that the users are either enabled or disabled. The Green Tick signifies that the user is enabled and the Red Cross signifies that the user is disabled and cannot function unless enabled.

To block a user, the best way is to simply change the tick from green to cross; this immediately disables the user account and he/she cannot be able to login from the front-end of the site. However, when it is turned back to green tick, the user can then login from the front-end.

Sending e-mails to a group of users

As the overall controller of the website, you can send an e-mail to a particular group of users. To do this:

1. Select **Tools**⟶**Mass Mail** from the top menu.

2. Type in your e-mail Subject and the body of the message into the input boxes.

3. Click on the **Parameters** icon to set some consistent details for every e-mail sent. This could be the name of the website or a signature at the end of the e-mail.

4. Furthermore, note some of the special e-mail settings:

    o **Mail to Child Groups**: Selecting this option means your e-mail will be sent to the user group selected and all of the child groups within. For example, if you send the e-mail to the Public Back-end group, the e-mail will be sent to all members of that group who are registered as Managers, Administrators, and Super Administrators

    o Send in **HTML Mode**: This means sending the e-mail with special code to allow the recipient's e-mail client to display any HTML content.

    o Group: Select the user group the e-mail should be sent to. Work in conjunction with the Mail to Child Group function.

o Recipients as **BCC**. Adds a copy to site e-mail: This means all recipients will be included as BCC (Blind Carbon Copy) entries. This means none of the recipients will see each other's e-mail address. See the image below:

5. Click the **Send Mail icon** to send the e-mail to your recipients.

Sending a Private Message to a User

You can send a private message to user. This message is only for the back-end users like the manager, Administrator and super Administrator. It is only sent within the area of the administrator panel only.

To send private message to other administrators, do the following:

- Go to **Tools** and click on the **Write Message** link.

- Select your recipient, enter the subject, and type in your message.

- Click **Send** and you are done!

This chapter has covered the user management within the Joomla! back-end interface which allows you to effectively create, manage and delete users from your website. There are many extensions that are available for Joomla! that can add more flavor to the functionality of the system.

Chapter Six

Working with the Media Manager

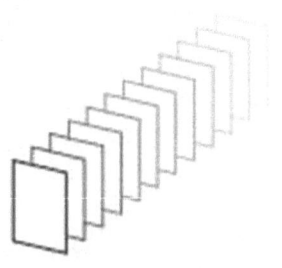

The Media Manager is a tool which is used for managing images that are used in a website. It makes working with images and inserting them into pages easier than uploading them and inserting them manually.

Joomla! has made everything simple in designing your website, and it is possible to do this because it takes care of uploading everything for you. Basically, this means that if you want to insert an image or a file link into one of your content pages, it doesn't require as much work as using FTP (file transfer protocol) to put the files on your web server.

How it works

You have to make sure that your Joomla! website is set up so that it can accept the files that you want to upload. Do the following steps:

1. Login to you Administrator Panel. Then go to the menu bar, select '**Site**' and then press '**Global Configuration**' from the list.

2. Click on the '**System**' tab. Then find the area titled 'Media Settings'. This is where all of the Media Manager settings are located.

Chapter Six - *Working with the Media Manager*

3. Find out what files you'll need to upload, and then make sure that their file extensions included in the 'Legal Extensions' list. Each file extension is separated by a comma.

✎ Joomla! has set up many file extensions for your media files. However, you might want to add some more.

4. Make sure that each of the files you're planning to upload will be small enough to transfer to the web server. The setting for 'Maximum Size' is set at 10Mb, a good size for most documents you might need to upload.

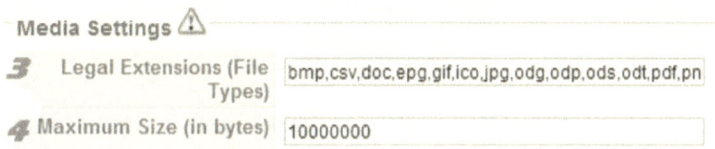

5. Other settings within the Media Manager setting should not be changed or touched.

6. Now click **Save**.

Making use of folders

The folders within the Media Manager can be used to sort images into categories. However, to create a new folder,

- Enter your desired folder name into the **Create Folder** text box and click on create folder button.

You can create a subfolder of a particular folder by navigating to that folder using the links on the left hand side of the page and then creating

109

the folder using the steps in the above paragraph.

(This means that you will have to click on the parent folder and then at the top right, type your desired folder name and click on the 'Create Folder' button).

To upload an image into a specific folder, navigate to that folder you wish to upload into using the links on the left hand side of the media manager page and follow these steps:

1. Open the folder you wish to upload an image into in the Media Manager.

2. Click on the **Choose File**. Here you will select the image form you local computer and then click on **Start Upload**.

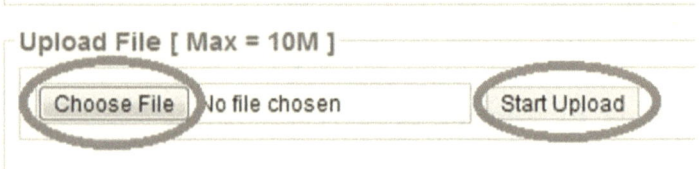

Uploading Images to Folders:

Usually when you are new to Joomla!, you would want to work with the Media Manager to upload an image or images. This can be done by clicking the **Choose Files** button and selecting the image you wish to upload, then clicking **Start Upload** as seen in picture above. The image should then appear on the main Media Manager page.

▶ Files with filenames that contain spaces or special characters cannot be uploaded.

Chapter Six - Working with the Media Manager

Adding images to pages of your Site

When you upload images to the Media Manger without using it in web pages of your website, it doesn't really have a value. Therefore, to add or insert image to your website pages you will require the following:

- Go to your Article Manager and select the article you wish you add an image to.

- Scroll down to the article page, you will see a button called **Image**.

- Click on it to select your image. You will see a popup like the following picture.

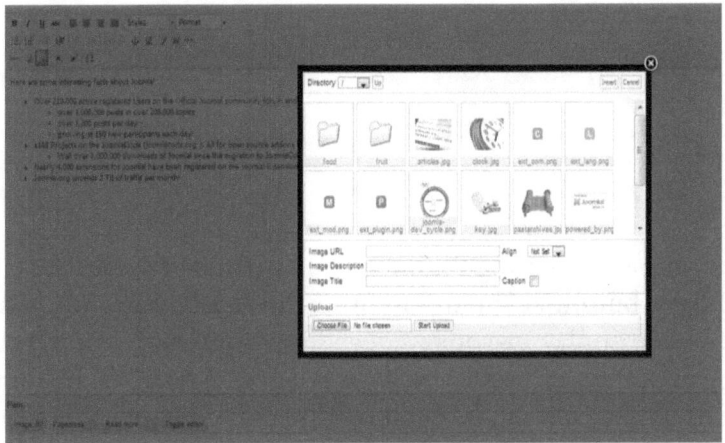

- Select the image that you wish to insert and fill in the image's details.

    You have already uploaded an image to the folder you created earlier. Now, you need to locate the folder within the Media Manager and select the image.

111

- **Image Description**: This is the text that will appear if the page is viewed by your website visitor whose browser t does not support images, or who has images turned off.

- **Align:** This is the location of the image on your page or article. The options are "left" and "right", for the left side and the right side of the page respectively.

- **Image Title**: This is the image caption; it is displayed below the image.

Assuming we choose the alignment of the image to left, it will display like this in the back-end of the site (article content area) when you edit the page.

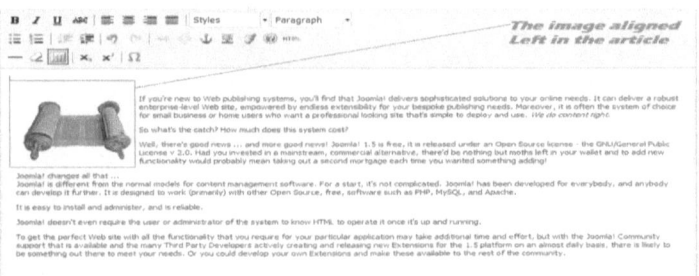

After editing and inserting the image, you will have to save it by clicking on the **Save** button at the top right of the article page. You will then have a better display of your webpage with the image on the top left of the page content. It looks better when you choose an alignment for the image in the content. Now, have a look at the front-end in the next picture.

Chapter Six - Working with the Media Manager

You are now done inserting an image to your webpage. The Media Manager is very important in building Joomla! websites as it enables you to insert images and other media files to your Joomla! site.

Chapter Seven

Usability, Accessibility and Web Standards

In this chapter we shall be looking at:

- Usability
- accessibility
- Search Engine Optimization
- W3C Web Standards

These are all phrases used to describe high quality WebPages in today's World Wide Web. In reality, there is a significant amount of overlap between them, and a web page that demonstrates the characteristics of one does so for all three. The easiest way to achieve these three goals is to do so using the framework laid out in the W3C web standards. You would like to ask yourself:

What makes a good website?

When you are developing a website, your website should have a "GOAL". It measures how "good" the website is and how successful it is in meeting that GOAL you have set. The goal for a social Networking Site will be very different to an e-commerce site; but notwithstanding, "good" websites share some common characteristics. However, in order to meet your goal, consider the following:

- ✓ First—Viewers have to find your site.
- ✓ They have to be able to view it easily.

- ✓ They have to be able to find what they want.

- ✓ Viewers must think your website is credible. You have to create a good impression.

There is significant overlap between these characteristics. The things that make a site easy to find are the same ones that make it viewable, navigable and credible. Take a look at each of the characteristics listed above to get a better view.

Viewers have to find your site

Most people on the web find a website through a search engine. According to Nielsen//NetRatings (2005), over 5 billion searches were carried out in October 2005, almost half of these were using Google. Unfortunately, "build it and they will come" is not true on the web. A website with no traffic stands little chance of achieving its goals. Potentially the most effective way to get traffic is through Search Engine Optimization (SEO). SEO are the strategies involved in increasing a website's search engine ranking where it appears in a search engine's results page.

Viewers have to be able to view your site easily

Various things can get in the way of someone trying to view your site for various reasons. Viewers with vision impairments, whether blind, color blind, old or simply viewing the site on a PDA/mobile phone need well laid out websites both in terms of organization (semantic layout) and graphical (white space/typography). Viewers on older computers might need sites that use little graphics or Flash. Many users for various reasons will browse your site with JavaScript turned off. All of these groups need a website that is accessible to them, and these viewers, according to some studies, can account for up to 30% of the population on the internet.

Viewers have to be able to find what they want

When a viewer can't find what they are looking for on your website easily, chances are they will leave and go elsewhere. Your website has to be useable. Studies vary in what they say about how long someone will take to figure out your website, but the figure quoted most often is about 8 seconds. More than 83% of Internet users are likely to leave a website if they feel they can't find what they're looking for, and 58% of visitors who experience usability problems don't come back (Source: Joomlashack).

Viewers must think your website is credible

If a viewer found your site, and figured out how to use it, they need to stay on it. "When a site lacks credibility, users are unlikely to remain on the site for long. They won't buy things, they won't register, and they won't return" (Makovsky, 2002 as cited by Baker, 2007).

What makes a site credible? In the same study, Stanford/Makovsky found that the "Design Look" or the site's overall design or look accounted for 46% of a site's credibility. This included layout, typography, white space, images, color schemes, and so on. This was followed by "Information Design/Structure" (28%) or how poorly the information fit together, as well as how hard it was to navigate the site to find things of interest. Many of the factors involved in being credible are the same for being accessible and usable.

SEO, Accessibility, Usability and Web Standards

Therefore, another way of looking at what makes a good website is to describe it in new terms. A good website is:

- ✓ Search engine optimized
- ✓ Accessible
- ✓ Usable

Chapter Seven - Usability, Accessibility and Web Standards

Many of the factors that make a site better at one of these also improve it in another; there are lots of overlap between them. For example, a site that is (x)html semantically structured (the xhtml explains the document, not how it looks), will be easily read in a screen reader by someone who has poor vision. It will also be easily read by a search engine spider. Google is effectively blind on how it reads your website. Another way of thinking about this is graphically.

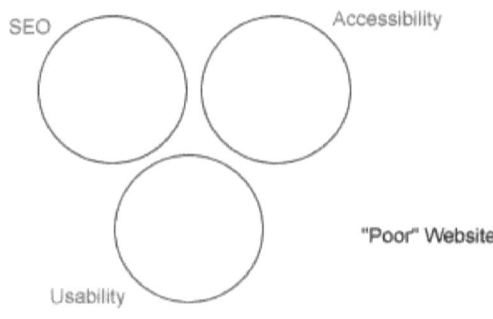

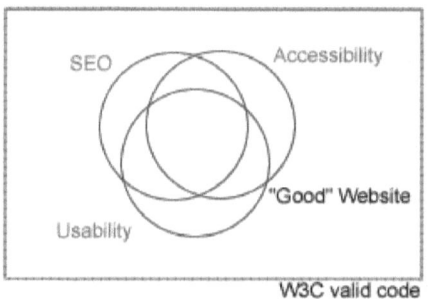

Source: Joomlashack

To have a good website, you will have lots of overlap. A framework is introduced by W3C valid code. A site that validates to the World Wide Web Consortium's (W3C) web standards has a much better foundation for making it accessible, usable and search-engine optimized. These are like building codes for a house. A website built with them is stronger and safer. You can check your pages with the W3C's HTML validation service for free. At its simplest, a site that meets W3C validation uses semantic (x)html and separates content from presentation using CSS.

Search Engine optimization SEO

Almost half of searches on the web are done with Google. What does it take to get a good SERP with this search engine? Patent #20050071741 or "Information Retrieval Based on Historical Data" (Google) describes over 118 factors that affect a web site's position in search engine's rankings. Some of the more important on-site factors are:

- Keywords in title tag, h1/h2 etc tags, alt text, URL and site links

- High keyword density in body, (content separated from presentation) preferably near beginning

- Small Pages<30k

- Themed pages

- Efficient internal link structure

The negative on-page factors include:

- Text presented in graphics

- Excessive JavaScript

- Excessive Flash

An organized usable page that is designed to be accessible will have a better chance of achieving high search engine result page (SERP). You can find more details about SEO at www.compassdesigns.net/articles/webmarketing/seo-guide.html.

✎ Details about Search Engine optimization is beyond the scope of this book.

Accessibility

Website accessibility is about making your site accessible to all Internet users regardless of what browsing technology they're using. Often accessibility is used in the context of blind users, but it is much more. It includes other vision-impaired users such as color blindness or the elderly, those using older browsers, users on mobiles phones or PDA's, or simply someone on a slow internet connection. A Good accessible web site will:

- ✓ Provide meaningful information in the title, h1/h2 and image alt tags
- ✓ Have the most useful information near the top
- ✓ Have pages that load fast
- ✓ Have meaningful link text
- ✓ Gives user control over pages, e.g. resizing text
- ✓ Include a text-based sitemap

Factors that make a page less accessible are:

- ✓ Text presented as graphics
- ✓ No alternative to JavaScript, particularly for navigation
- ✓ No alternative to Flash content

A page designed to be accessible will also be highly usable and include many of the factors for SEO.

Usability

Classically usability is defined as "a quality attribute that assesses how easy user interfaces are to use". Steve Krug of "Don't Make Me Think" uses the example from his wife, "*if I have to think more I just don't use it as much*". Another quote illustrates the importance of usability, albeit from a commercial perspective: "*Homepages are the most valuable real estate in the world. Each year, companies and individuals funnel millions of dollars through a space that's not even a square foot in size. . . Corporate homepages are the most valuable real estate in the world. Space on a big company's homepage is worth about 1,300 times as much as land in the business districts of Tokyo.*" (Jakob Nielsen on Usability and Web Design)

Usable pages:

- o Employ scannable text and meaningful sub-headings.
- o Use meaningful graphics, not just pictures of models.
- o Have small graphics whenever possible to reduce download time.
- o Avoid using graphics as links or content.
- o Have a well-organized site.
- o Use text-based navigation.

To describe negative factors of usability, here are some of Jakob Nielson's Top Web Design Mistakes: http://www.useit.com/alertbox/designmistakes.html

- o Frozen font sizes and low contrast between text and background.
- o Non-standard JavaScript links

- Flash navigation.

- Browser Incompatibility

- Frozen layouts with fixed page widths

- Page titles with low search engine visibility

An analysis of web design award winners (http://www.webphil.com/sdwanalysis.htm) came to the conclusion that, "If your goal is to win Web Awards, then it seems that you should design an aesthetically good looking Web site at the expense of usability. The Web site will look good, but will be slow and difficult to use for some viewers. But if your goal is to sell products or services, then we should look at the Web sites that succeed in this goal. Amazon is the leader when it comes to selling products, Yahoo is the most popular search directory, AOL has millions of users, and Microsoft, the most successful software company today. What do their Web sites have in common? As we have seen, they all focus on usability. The all have fast and easy to use Web sites." (Mangilit, 2002)

W3C Web Standards

You may have seen words such as "web standards" or "CSS", but what exactly are they? "These technologies, which is called web standards are carefully designed to deliver the greatest benefits to the greatest number of web users while ensuring the long-term viability of any document published on the Web" (source: webstandards.org/about/).

To facilitate your understanding on where web standards came from, some history is helpful. Many web pages are actually designed for older browsers. Why? Browsers have continually evolved since the www started. New ones have appeared and old ones have disappeared (remember Netscape?). Another complicating factor is that different browser makers (like Microsoft) tend to have their browsers interpret html/xhtml in slightly different ways (TJ Baker, 2007). This has lead to web designers having to design their websites to support older browsers rather than new ones. It's often decided that the web page needs to appear properly to these "legacy" browsers.

Web standards put into place a common set of "rules" for all web browsers to use to show a web page. The main organization pushing these standards is the World Wide Web Consortium (WC3), who's Director, Tim Berners-Lee has the distinction of actually inventing the World Wide Web in 1989.

Ask five designers what web standards are and you will get five answers. But most agree that they are based on the following:

- **Valid code, whether html or xhtml (or others)**

The standards outlined for the code that makes a web page have been developed to achieve consistency. It's easy to check your code at validator.w3.org. However, make sure you use the correct DOCTYPE when you try and validate your code. These points described valid Joomla! doctype.

- **Semantically Correct Code**

We mentioned before that being semantic means that the (x)html in the web page describes only content, not presentation. To be exact, this means structured organization of h1/h2 etc tags and only using tables for tabular data, not to layout a web page.

- **Cascading Style Sheets (CSS)**

This is basically related to having semantic (well organized) code, using cascading style sheets to control the look and layout of your web page. Cascading Style Sheets (CSS) is a simple mechanism for adding style (e.g. fonts, colors, and spacing) to Web documents. (www.w3.org/Style/CSS/). They exist parallel to the (x)html code and so let you completely separate content (semantic code) from presentation (CSS). The best example of this is CSS Zen Garden, a site where the same semantic xhtml is shaped in different and unique ways with different CSS. The result is pages that look very different but have the same core content. The following table shows how these factors are related:

	SEO	Accessibility	Usability
Positive	<ul><li>Keywords in URL, title tag, h1/h2 etc tags, alt text and site links</li><li>High keyword density in body, (content separated from presentation) preferably near beginning</li><li>Small Pages <30k</li><li>Themed pages</li><li>Efficient internal link structure</li></ul>	<ul><li>Provide meaningful information in the title, h1/h2 and image alt tags</li><li>Have the most useful information near the top</li><li>Have pages that load fast</li><li>Have meaningful link text</li><li>Gives user control over pages, e.g. resizing text</li><li>Include a text-based sitemap</li></ul>	<ul><li>Employ scannable text and meaningful sub-headings</li><li>Use meaningful graphics, not just pictures of models.</li><li>Have small graphics whenever possible to reduce download time.</li><li>Avoid using graphics as links or content</li><li>Have a well-organized site</li><li>Use text-based navigation</li></ul>
Negative	<ul><li>Text presented in graphics</li><li>Excessive JavaScript</li><li>Excessive Flash</li></ul>	<ul><li>Text presented as graphics</li><li>No alternative to JavaScript, particularly for navigation</li><li>No alternative to Flash content</li></ul>	<ul><li>Frozen font sizes and low contrast between text and background.</li><li>Non-standard JavaScript links</li><li>Flash navigation.</li><li>Browser Incompatibility</li><li>Frozen layouts with fixed page widths</li><li>Page titles with low search engine visibility</li></ul>

The table above shows a significant overlap. Clearly to have a site that is both search engine optimized, accessible, and usable, you need to make sure that you have:

- Good semantic markup
- Small page sizes
- Efficient and meaningful link structure
- Meaningful graphics and no graphics as text
- Small amount of JavaScript or flash

The most effective way to achieve these is to design web pages to current W3C standards. Using CSS in particular to separate content for presentation is highly effective in meeting these goals.

What does this mean for a Joomla! Website?

Looking at the above criteria, all of these factors are currently controlled by the template designer, not the core of the Joomla! itself. The designer can create a template that incorporates good semantics, or small pages sizes. Sometimes Joomla! does have issues where it outputs content in tables and is not using useful semantic headers. However, advanced Joomla! template designers are able to overcome this drawback and produce a template that results in a site that is accessible, usable and search engine optimized.

Chapter Eight

Using Templates and Extensions in Joomla!

A template is the type of Joomla! extension that changes the way your site looks. There are two types of templates: Front-end Templates and Back-end Templates. However changing the style of your Joomla! website is very easy through templates. When you install a template, the Menu, Modules and Contents are still same but the colors and styles will be different. There are many site devoted to free Joomla! templates and you surely can download as many as you want; all you have to do is go to a search engine and type in *Free Joomla! Template* and many free templates will appear. Alternatively, you can use the Joomla! forums for guidance on how to get a Joomla! template. When you finally get a Template that you like, download it to your computer, it will come in a "Zip File" when you have the zip file, now go and Install it to your Joomla! site.

Installing Joomla! Template

Do the following steps:

1. Log into the back-end of your site 'localhost/your-sitename/administrator/' or 'localhost/learnjoomla/administrator' (for the purpose of this book) or (*www.your-site.com*/administrator/) when you are using the live host.

2. Click on: Extensions⟶Install/Uninstall

Chapter Eight - Using Templates and Extensions in Joomla!

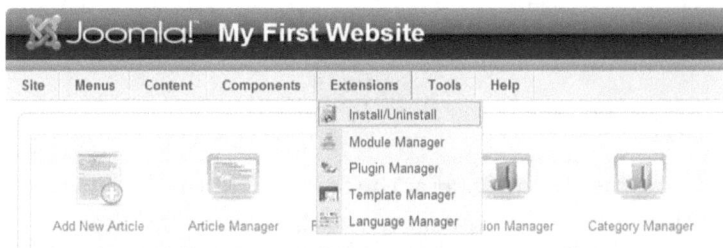

You see the page "Extension Manager". From here, you can install your Templates, Plugins, Modules, Components and Languages. You have three options:

- Upload Package File-(select a package from your PC, upload and install it).

- Install from Directory-(enter the path where the package is located on your server).

- Install from URL-(enter the URL to the package).

We will use the first method to install the Template as it is most suitable.

3. Select the package from your PC and click the button **Upload File & Install**

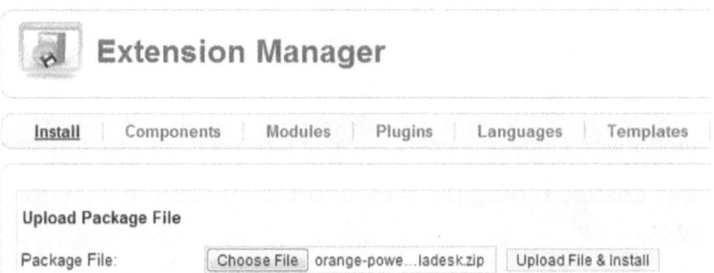

If the package contains no errors, you are done and you will get a success message. In case of error, contact the template provider or ask questions in Joomla! Forum.

129

4. Go to Extension →Template Manager. You will see the entire installed template.

5. Select the Newly installed Template.

6. Click the 'Yellow' Star at the top right of the Template manager. The template is now set as the default for the site.

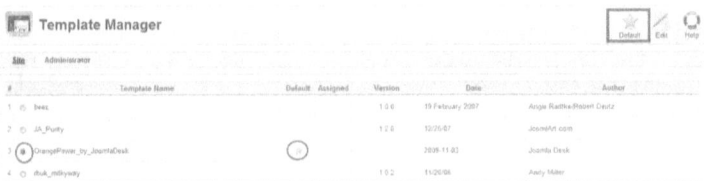

7. Click preview to see the changes on your site front-end.

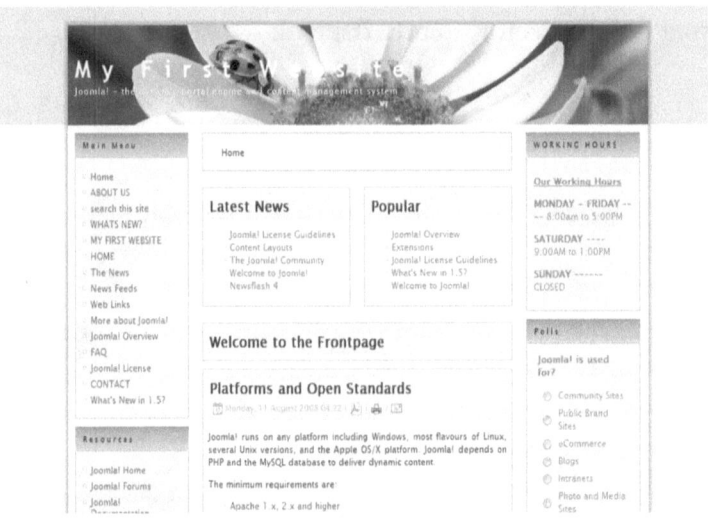

You will notice that all the Content and Modules are the same. When a template is changed, only the look and feel of the site changes but not the contents.

There are times when you install and change the template of your site, some Modules and Components disappear. This is because every template has its design and module positions. The best way to organize your site is to see the various module positions of the template; this will help you in organizing your site.

Chapter Eight - Using Templates and Extensions in Joomla!

To view the template Module positions from the back-end of your Joomla! site, simply

1. Go to Extension──➤Template Manager.

2. Select and click on the Default Template. (That is the template u are using for your site).

3. Click on Preview on the top right of the Template: [Edit] page.

That the preview here is different from previewing the site in another browser.

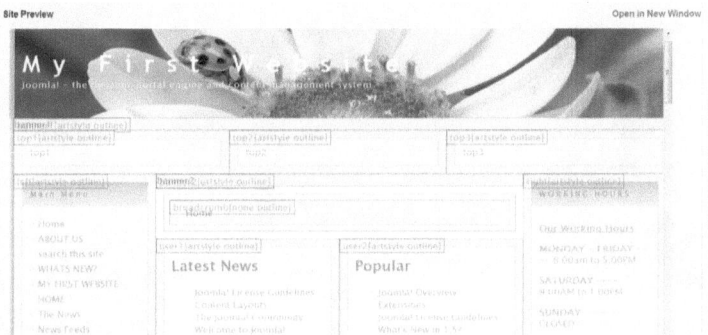

You will see something like this which shows the various Module positions available for the template, and that will further help you to re-organize your Joomla! website. Click back button at the top right of the page and click Save.

You can also assign different templates to various menu items. You can contact the template provider for more on this. Some template cannot be assigned to different menu items.

Using Extensions in Joomla!

Most functionality in Joomla! is provided through Extension to the core code. While Joomla! has different extensions pre-installed, you can always add more to get more features. In this section you will learn about the Extension manager. An "Extension" is a software package that extends your Joomla! installation in some way. A small selection of extensions is included with the default Joomla! installation but many more are available at the Joomla! Extensions Directory at http://extensions.joomla.org/.

Now, let's go to the extension Manager and describe the different extension types. To do this, Go to Extension⟶ Install/uninstall.

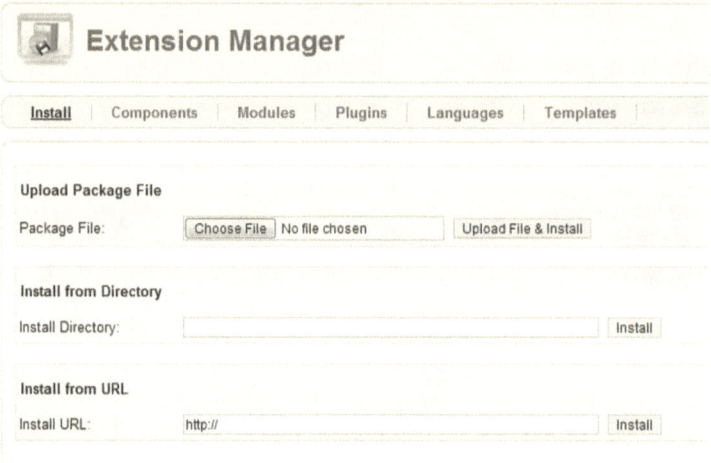

From this screen, you can install any type of Extension. When you have an Extension ready to install, click **Choose file** to find it on your computer. Once you find it, click **Upload File/Install.**

The "Install from Directory" option is an advanced tool that you can use if you having trouble installing from file; normally you won't need to use this.

Finally, you can "Install from URL "if the Zip file is available on a public website, you can Paste the address here and click Install. Now let's take a look at the different types of extensions.

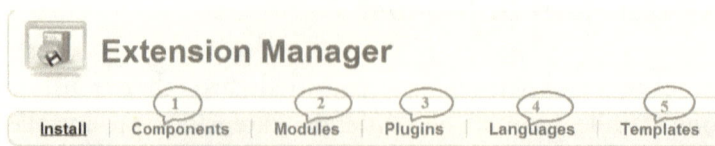

1. Components: Components provide the main functionality for every page in Joomla! only one component load with every page.

2. Modules: These are small pieces of content that you can place around your site page some example of pre defined Modules are the Breadcrumbs, Polls, Login Form and Search. You can have as many modules as you want on your page and you can publish certain Modules to specific pages.

3. Plugins: These provide a variety of functionality in Joomla! and some functions are visible in the site; examples are the buttons used in the contents. However, some functionalities are not visible.

4. Languages: These translate the Joomla! user interface into other languages. You can install this extension to translate the interface of your site.

5. Templates: These control the feel and look of your site. You can have more than one template on your site with one Template set as the Default and another Template set to only display on certain pages. Five different extension types work together to generate every page in Joomla!. To get more features for Joomla!, install more extensions. More extensions can be installed through the Extension Manager which allows you to upload a **Zip file** from your computer. Install from a folder or simply install form the URL.

Conclusion

You have done a fabulous job which you might not yet realize now. Your First Joomla! website is up and running. This book has shown you that building your website with Joomla! is a three—step process. First, you customize the layout, then you add content, and finally you add additional functionalities such as the contact form, poll and the search components to your site.

Before you create content pages in your site, you create the containers they belong to; that is if you have many content pages in your site. These containers are called sections (which is the top level) and categories (which is the second level). You may create uncategorized articles if you need some contents pages that do not fit in categories. This usually is for content that stand on their own like the "About us" Page in most websites.

This book also shows you that no content will be visible on your website without a menu link pointing at it. However, you add items to the front page of your site by simply changing their front page setting. You can change the order of the contents in the Front page Manager and will be presented accordingly.

You can add as much extra functionalities through the components and the extensions. Example of this is the Poll component that allows users to vote on your site and view the result instantly.

This book followed the easy, fast, simple and step-by-step approach and used only the basic capabilities of the system, leaving most settings at their default values. As you explore and put Joomla! into practice, you will master it, creating much bigger, complex and sophisticated websites.

A very big THANK YOU for reading this Book. Remember that Joomla! can be used for much more than Content Management. It is, no doubt, a powerful web application that can simply be used to build anything from simple home pages to complex corporate websites. Joomla! has a directory that has currently more than 8000 extensions ready for your website and there are countless templates both (free and commercial) available across the internet. Now that you know how to use Joomla! Go build a website! For more information and latest update about Joomla! visit www.joomla.org.

Appendix

Appendix A: Exporting & Importing Joomla! Database from your computer

By now, you should know that Joomla! 1.5 consists of TWO components, the Joomla! files and the Database. These files and folders of your Joomla! applications contain the scripts and core application codes, while the Joomla! Database contains all records of your website such as articles, sections, categories, images, etc.

To perform this task, I assume you have WAMP web server installed. So, click on your server icon in the bottom right of your taskbar and click on the **phpMyAdmin**; you should see a screen that looks like this:

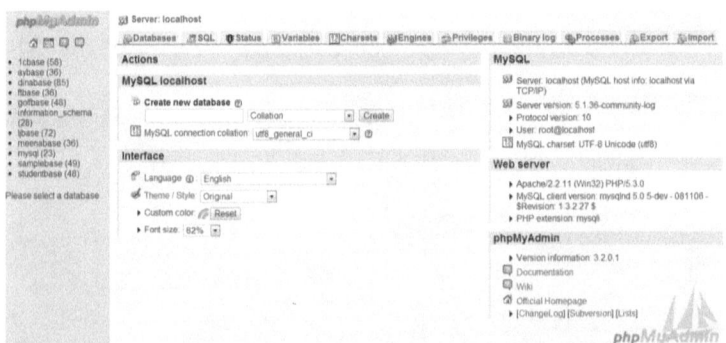

This process is for the localhost Database transfer from one PC to another PC. Do this if you want to continue building your website on another Computer. However, if you want to transfer your database from your personal computer to another host company, you will have to contact them for further assistance.

You should see a list of the databases available on the top left column. Click on the link to your Joomla! database, i.e. the database that you wish to export. In this example, the database is "ljbase". Once you have clicked on your Joomla! database, you will be shown a screen like this:

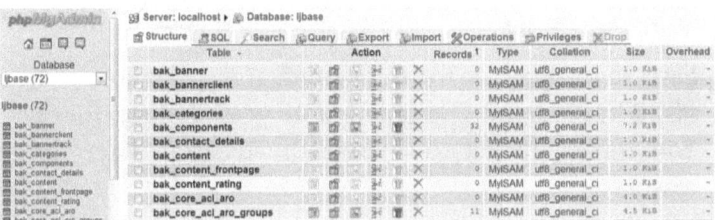

Make sure the database you choose is the right one for the Joomla! files and folders, i.e., your website. Do not delete any of the tables. Click on the tab labeled "Export", and you will be shown a screen like this:

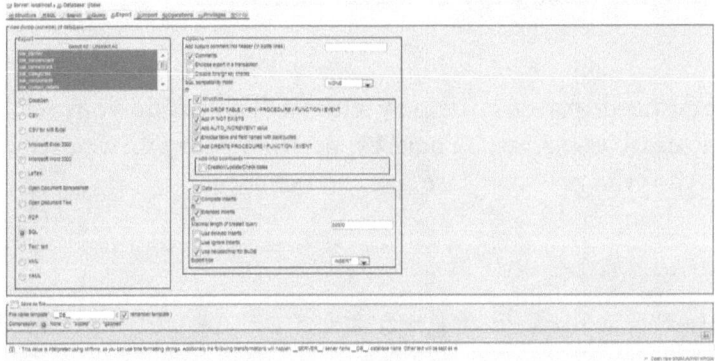

Exporting Process

Let me show you a trick here. Follow these simple steps, and you will have your database exported to an SQL file and saved on your PC.

1. Select all of your Joomla! tables from the list of tables. It is selected by default, so leave it as it is.

2. In the list of export types, make sure "SQL" is selected. It is selected by default. (This makes it easier to re-import your data later.)

3. Leave your "SQL" options as they are.

4. Make sure **Save as file** is checked at the bottom of the page.

5. Click the button labeled **Go** in the bottom right of the page.

6. Save your ".sql" file to your system and make note of where you saved it. I recommend saving it on your desktop for easy access. You might decide to change the location later for security reason.

You are done with the export. You should now have a file on your system that is an exact copy of your Joomla! database.

Importing the saved copy into a new database

You'll first need to create the new, empty database on your server. Use the same database name you have exported to your PC, we used "ljbase" earlier. After the new database has been created:

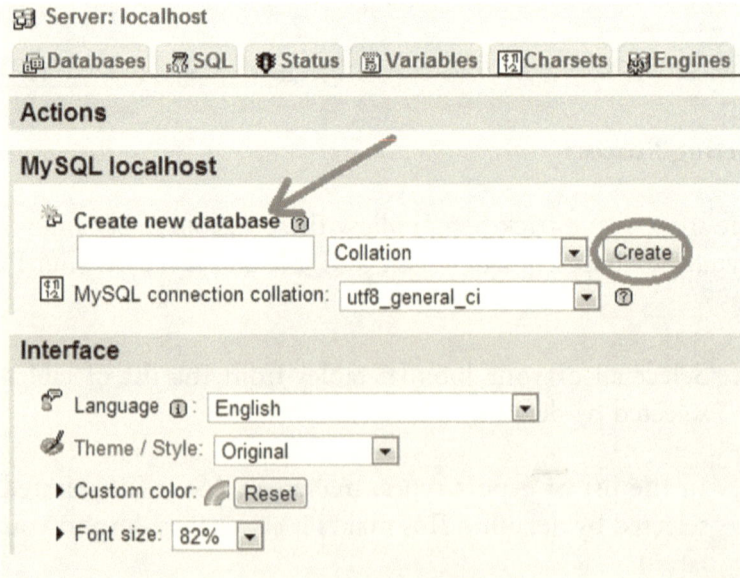

1. Go to phpMyAdmin page via your WAMP server (localhost).

2. Click the database name on the top left-hand side of the page.

3. Select the Import tab.

4. Click the Browse button under "File to import", then select the database file from your computer.

5. Click Go to import the database.

💡 If you see a "No database selected" error, it's probably because you forgot to first click on the database name in the left-hand column.

In this section, you have learned how to export your Joomla! database on your personal computer, have it saved (for backup) and import it to another Computer. This can only be executed if you have localhost on your computer, if you have problems transferring your Joomla! 1.5 by yourself, ask your host company for assistance.

Appendix B: Key Resources

Joomla—http://www.joomla.org/

WAMP (Windows)—For more information, visit http://www.wampserver.com

Download Joomla! 1.5. x—http://www.joomla.org/download.html

Joomla! Extensions Directory: Find an extension—http://extensions.joomla.org/

Joomla! Forums: Get support.—http://forum.joomla.org/

Joomla! Forums—http://forum.joomla.org/viewforum.php?f=429

Technical Requirements: Get ready to install—http://www.joomla.org/technical-requirements.html

Joomla! Core Features—http://help.joomla.org/ghop/feb2008/task020/Joomla!%20Core%20Features%20V1.2.pdf

Joomlashack—http://www.joomlashack.com/

JoomSpirit—http://www.joomspirit.com/Free-templates/Itemid-126.html

Joomla24 Templates—http://www.joomla24.com/

Joomlaxe1.5 free templates—http://www.joomlaxe.com/

Free Templates—http://www.joomlashack.com/products/free-joomla-templates

Professional Joomla! Templates—http://www.joomlashack.com/products/professional-joomla-templates

Jakob Nielsen's Website—http://www.useit.com/

Joel Mangilit—http://www.webphil.com/sdwanalysis.htm

JOOMLA HOSTING

SiteGround Web Hosting company—http://www.siteground.com/

GreenGeeks—http://www.greengeeks.com/

justhost.com—http://www.justhost.com/

FatCow—http://www.fatcow.com/fatcow/special-promo.bml?LinkName=No_Name

Hostgator—http://www.hostgator.com/

Appendix C: Look who's using Joomla!

Jaguar—http://www.jaguar.gr

Monaco yacht show—http://www.monacoyachtshow.com

Barnes & noble—https://nookdeveloper.barnesandnoble.com

U.K ministry of defense—http://www.stabilisationunit.gov.uk

McDonald's—www.mcdonaldsarabia.com

Pizza hut—http://www.pizzahut.fr

The European Union—http://www.eurunion.org

university of alabama at birmingham—http://uab.edu

And many more at http://joomlagov.info/

ABOUT THE AUTHOR

Abdulkadir Shehu is a practicing Joomla! trainer in Kuala Lumpur, Malaysia.

He holds a BSc. (Hons) in Business Information System at University of East London. Having worked in the web design industry for many years, he has been educating colleagues, friends and clients about the effectiveness of using Joomla! in website development.

Mr. Shehu has conducted Joomla! training for companies, business owners, students, and individuals to name just a few, to help them build and sustain their Joomla! websites. When not working, he takes pleasure in making new friends and loves sharing his knowledge with others. He is a Nigerian but currently lives in Kuala Lumpur, Malaysia. This is his first book.

www.ingramcontent.com/pod-product-compliance
Lightning Source LLC
Chambersburg PA
CBHW032023170526
45157CB00002B/826